THE COST OF SILENCE

The Churches Role In The Destruction of A Nation

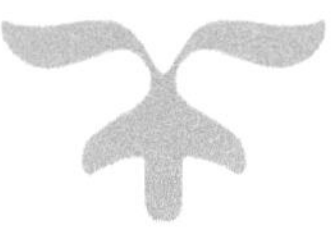

John L Gagne

that are incurred as a result of the use of the information contained within this document, including, but not limited to, errors, omissions, or inaccuracies.

Table of Contents

Acknowledgements

First and foremost, I give thanks to God for His endless love, grace, and guidance in my life. His faithfulness has been my foundation throughout this journey, giving me the strength, clarity, and perseverance to bring this book to completion. Without Him, none of this would be possible. To Him be all the glory.

I want to extend special gratitude to my friend Mary Ann McCafferty, whose enthusiasm and encouragement meant the world to me. You were the biggest fan of my work in my videos, and your belief in what I create has been a constant source of motivation.

A sincere thank you to my friend Suliman Bakri, your encouragement and belief in this project were invaluable.

Finally, I am deeply grateful to my wife Eden, and my son Ravi, Your unwavering support and help with the responsibilities at home allowed me the time and focus needed to write. Your love, patience, and encouragement were essential to completing this journey. This book would not have been possible without you.

Thank you all for being part of this journey with me.

Preface

In January of 2024, a deep unmistakable burden settled in my heart. It was as though a switch had been flipped in my mind, and everything seemed clear.

You could say that driving a truck or working a blue collar job is just where I happen to be at this moment in time, it's not the whole picture of who I am or who I'm becoming. I am an eternal being, part of God's grand design, and while I don't yet know all the things He'll call me to do, I know this phase is just one chapter in a much bigger story. My faith in Christ and my biblical worldview have been constants for decades now in my life. I've spent years reading and hearing the Word, listening to preachers proclaim God's limitless power. They've reminded me time and again that when we pray according to His will, He will move. That truth keeps me anchored, guiding how I navigate both the present moment and the unknown future God has for me.

So, here's the question, If this is true, why wouldn't we be involved in shaping the future of our nation? Isn't this country supposed to be for the people and by the people? This country was founded on biblical principles, and that foundation is what made it great. The Pilgrims, you could say, were driven by a righteous anger against tyranny and injustice, they were in essence, "angry church people" in the best sense. But somewhere along the line, the church started to withdraw from public life. Slowly, we've grown quiet, and that passivity has allowed evil to thrive in our nation.

Who needs righteous indignation when you have the peace that passes understanding... and moral responsibility. It's a strange new kind of evil, though not new at all. I've come to call it, piety paralysis, where christians are so preoccupied with piety that they forget that faith without works is dead. We talk about prayer but refuse to take action. And while prayer is vital, evil delights in those who think prayer alone absolves them from any responsibility to confront it. This could also be called, innocent indifference, where ignorance is not bliss, but a virtue. But no matter what you call it, it's wrong. Dead wrong.

Five months after that January moment of clarity, I completed the video project that had been weighing on my heart. I called it, The Silence Of The Church.

But when I released the video, the response I got was eerily fitting for the topic.

From the church people that I rub shoulders with, there was mostly silence. Most of them had no interest in even watching it. When someone did watch it, the feedback I got was often criticism. Some didn't like my tone and the anger I expressed. Yeah, why get angry about millions of dead unborn babies and the sexualization of our children right? Some reminded me that the bible says the world is going to get worse before the end, therefore my video in essence was pointless. I'm aware of what the bible says too, but I couldn't find the part about how we're supposed to stick our head in the sand and do nothing about it. Others thought I was promoting sinful behavior from my talk about alcohol consumption.

 Curious, none of my critics are lining up to battle against the strongholds of sin for the betterment of society and our nation. They do absolutely nothing while feeling thoroughly justified. It's the type of evil that knows all the right bible verses about God's power but conveniently forgets them when actual action is required.

Charles Spurgeon once said, "boldhearted men are always called mean spirited by cowards." And that's the heart of the issue isn't it? When you dare to speak the truth, especially about the tough issues, you'll be labeled, criticized, and dismissed. But I don't care about the labels. The stakes are too high. Our silence has come at a great cost, and unless we find the courage to break that silence, the future of this nation hangs in the balance.That's why I wrote this book, to challenge the church to speak up and take action before it's too late.

The churches I attended were what most would call good churches. We learned the Bible and salvation through the finished work of Christ on the cross. Sure, I didn't see eye to eye with everything, like the King James was the only legitimate Bible version, or the claim that Jesus made grape juice instead of wine at the wedding at Cana. But beyond those quirks, I thought we were solid. After all, compared to the churches preaching truly bizarre doctrines, ours looked pretty sound. We had plenty of Bible studies, ice cream socials, and potlucks. We are frequently told, Baptist like to eat. No alcohol of course, but gluttony seemed to get a free pass.

We were great at keeping prayer lists for people in the hospital, the elderly, and anyone facing life's troubles. There were cards, visits, and casseroles. And often, we were reminded that God is all powerful, all knowing, and that if we prayed in line with His will, He would act. We heard about how much God hates sin, the death of the innocent, and the corruption of young minds. So it took me a while, but it finally clicked, If God is all powerful, and we are His people, shouldn't we be the most powerful force in the world? Shouldn't we be tearing down high places, passing just laws, and opposing evil wherever it shows up?

Instead, the same people who spoke of God as being all powerful also insisted, there's really nothing we can do about the sin in the world. Say what? They were quick to point out that the Bible says things will get worse before the end. But I've read my Bible too, and I must've missed the part where we're told to sit quietly with our heads in the sand, waiting for things to implode. It doesn't add up, how can we claim to serve an all powerful God while acting like powerless spectators?

When I think of how this country was founded by godly men, I feel a deep burden. How did we get from that legacy to this? I can't understand how we, who claim to believe in the power of God, are so unwilling to fight against the evil surrounding us. Jesus said if we stay silent, the rocks will cry out. And honestly, I feel that in the core of my being. I want to cry out, I have to cry out. I realize not everyone is willing to take a stand. Just like not everyone was ready to fight the Redcoats. Some folks just wanted to be left alone under British rule. But it wasn't those people who secured our freedom. It was the ones who stood up, fought, and sacrificed that made the difference. And that's what we're called to do.

Comfortable christianity has paralyzed the church, and it's not right. I can't find a church in my area that preaches the full gospel, speaks up against evil, and acts on it. But I know there are others out there who do. My voice and influence may be small, but it's what I got, and I want to do something with it. Whether it's through my videos, conversations, or this book, I want to join with others, because courage is contagious.

Yes, the Bible does say the world is going to get worse before the end, but I believe that's happening precisely because of God's people, the church. It's not some unstoppable force we're powerless to prevent. It's the result of the very ones entrusted with God's truth doing nothing. When the church refuses to speak out, evil fills the void. The decline we're seeing isn't just prophecy unfolding, it's a consequence of our complacency.

In Revelation 3:16, Jesus has some stern words for the church, "Because you are lukewarm, neither hot nor cold, I am about to vomit you out of my mouth!" That warning isn't just for some ancient congregation, it's for us. It's for a church that's become too comfortable, too passive, and too indifferent.

Introduction

This book is born out of a sense of urgency, a call that has been growing louder in my spirit. It's a call not just for me, but for all of us, especially the church, to wake up. In the pages that follow, I will take you on a journey through history, present day realities, and the looming threats we face as a nation. But this isn't just a history lesson or a catalog of political grievances. It's a wake up call to confront a troubling truth. America, the land of the free, the home of the brave, is in decline. And the key reason in my opinion is the silence of the church.

From its earliest days, this nation was built on christian principles. The Mayflower Compact, signed by the Pilgrims in 1620, was not just a political agreement, it was a covenant made with God. The founders of this country understood that true freedom comes from submission to divine authority, and that government, like the people it serves, must be guided by moral truth. America's founding documents reflect this belief, from the Declaration of Independence's acknowledgment of a creator to the constitution's framework for justice and liberty. These principles, rooted in a biblical worldview, made America great.

But over time, something has shifted. The church, once a powerful voice in public discourse, has been receding from the very arenas where its influence is most needed. We have allowed our voices to be drowned out by secular ideologies and have retreated from engaging with the culture. We've chosen the comfort of our pews over the confrontation of public sin. As a result, the moral foundations that once underpinned this country are eroding, and our freedoms are slipping away.

Throughout this book, you'll read quotes from notable figures past and present who warned of the dangers we now face. Their words serve as guideposts, reminding us of the consequences of inaction. One of the gravest threats we must confront is the issue of abortion. Over 60 million unborn children have lost their lives since Roe v. Wade, and the silence from the church on this matter is deafening. If we truly believe that life is sacred, why have we been so reluctant to defend it?

Our freedoms are being eroded in other ways too. The steady march of government overreach, the rise of censorship, and the increasing hostility toward those who hold biblical values are chipping away at the liberty that was once our birthright. But this is not new. History offers a sobering parallel in Nazi Germany, where the church remained largely silent as evil took hold. The cost of that silence was unimaginable. And now, in our time we are seeing similar patterns, moral decay, government tyranny, and a passive church that refuses to engage.

One of the most dangerous ideologies we face today is Marxism, which has infiltrated not only our government but also our educational institutions. Our schools and universities, once places where free thought and debate flourished, are now breeding grounds for radical leftist agendas. Marxism is anti God at its core, and yet, it has found fertile soil in the minds of our youth. As christians, we have a responsibility to stand against this destructive ideology, but once again, we've largely remained silent.

We'll also explore the issue of illegal immigration and the rise of "no go zones" in various parts of the country, places where law and order are all but abandoned, and where dangerous ideologies take root. These areas are symptomatic of a broader problem, the breakdown of law and order, and the abandonment of biblical justice in favor of lawlessness.

This book will address these pressing issues, but it won't stop there. I believe in pointing to the problem, but I also believe in offering solutions. We cannot afford to end this discussion in despair or hopelessness. There is something we can and must do about the state of our nation. The church has been silent for far too long, and it's time for us to find our voice again.

We'll talk about what we, as believers and as citizens, can do to turn the tide. We'll discuss practical ways to get involved in the political process, to engage with our communities, and to boldly speak truth in love. It won't be easy, and it won't be without opposition, but if we want to see real change, we must act. Faith without works is dead, and silence in the face of evil is itself evil.

The Cost of Silence is more than just a book, it's a rallying cry. It's an invitation to examine where we've gone wrong as a nation and as the body of Christ, and it's a challenge to stand up and make things right. The price of our passivity is too high. Our freedoms, our children's futures, and the soul of this nation are at stake. Let us not be remembered as the generation that watched in silence while America fell. Let us be the generation that took a stand, spoke out, and fought for the truth.

This is a fight worth engaging in, and it's not too late to turn the tide. The question is, will we have the courage to speak up?

CHAPTER 1:

A Covenant with God

*E*xploring America's founding on biblical principles, The Mayflower Compact.

When the Pilgrims set sail on the Mayflower in 1620, they weren't simply seeking new lands or running from persecution, they were on a divine mission. These men and women, driven by their faith, understood that their journey was about more than survival or economic opportunity. It was about establishing a society founded on the principles of the bible, a society where God's laws could take root and flourish. The Mayflower Compact, signed in the cramped confines of their ship, was not just a political agreement. It was a sacred covenant. A covenant not only with one another but with God Himself.

"In the name of God, Amen."

These are the first words of the Mayflower Compact, a document many consider to be the cornerstone of the American experiment. At a time when survival was uncertain, when the vast wilderness stretched before them, these Pilgrims recognized that they were part of something bigger than themselves. They were entering into a new phase of history, and they saw their arrival in the new world as part of God's divine plan. They had a mission to create a society that would honor Him, obey His laws, and serve as a "city upon a hill" a beacon of light to the world.

The compact they signed wasn't long or complex. It was a simple, straightforward statement of their intent to govern themselves in accordance with biblical principles. But its significance cannot be overstated. It was the first governing document of its kind in the new world, and it set the stage for the birth of the United States. The signers understood that a society's foundation is only as strong as the principles upon which it stands. For them, those principles were found in scripture.

In the book "Of Plymouth Plantation" by William Bradford, the Pilgrims' journey on the Mayflower and the signing of the Mayflower Compact are described with a deep sense of purpose and divine providence. Bradford explains that the Pilgrims, recognizing that they were entering a new and unknown land without an established government, realized the need for a framework of self governance. They crafted the Mayflower Compact as a means of ensuring order and unity within the colony. This agreement, a covenant between the settlers and God, was foundational in establishing a sense of community and responsibility to one another.

Bradford wrote about the challenges that the Pilgrims faced upon landing in a new world. They were far from the original Virginia territory where they had intended to settle, and they had no legal authority to govern. The Compact became a solution to this problem, creating an early form of governance that allowed the settlers to govern themselves according to the "general good" of the colony. The Mayflower Compact was simple, but profound in its implications, it established a government based on the consent of the governed, with laws enacted for the common good, rather than through a monarch's decree.

In "Mayflower, A Story of Courage, Community, and War" by Nathaniel Philbrick, the Mayflower Compact is seen as a pragmatic solution to the Pilgrims' immediate needs. The book emphasizes that many of the men aboard the Mayflower were not Separatists, and there was a fear that without a unifying document, factions might tear the fledgling colony apart. Philbrick details how the Compact was not only a social contract but also a safeguard against anarchy. It united the settlers under a common cause and laid the groundwork for future political structures in America.

Philbrick also draws attention to the Compact's historical significance as the first governing document in what would become the United States. Though it was not a constitution in the modern sense, the Mayflower Compact's focus on self rule and collective responsibility influenced the future development of democratic principles in America. Its simplicity belied its long lasting impact on how Americans would come to view governance , not as something imposed from above, but as something agreed upon by the people.

These books highlight the importance of the Mayflower Compact not only as a functional agreement for the survival of the colony but as a stepping stone in the development of the American democratic Republic. The Pilgrims' emphasis on a government that was for the benefit of all laid the groundwork for the future ideals of liberty and equality that would define the nation.

This idea of America as a nation under God is woven into the fabric of our history. From the earliest colonial charters to the Declaration of Independence, the recognition of a higher authority has always been central to the American experiment. The founding fathers, though differing in their specific religious beliefs, shared a common understanding, that the freedoms and rights they were enshrining were not granted by government but by God. This conviction is made clear in the Declaration of Independence, where Thomas Jefferson writes that all men are endowed by their Creator with certain unalienable rights.

It's important to pause here and consider the radical nature of this idea. Throughout much of human history, rights and freedoms were bestowed by kings or rulers. The idea that these rights were inherent, given by God and not subject to the whims of men, was revolutionary. And it's this idea that made America unique. Our nation wasn't just built on a collection of laws or political philosophies, it was built on a foundation of biblical truth.

But this foundation didn't spring up overnight. It was the result of generations of struggle, prayer, and perseverance. The Pilgrims, with their Mayflower Compact, planted the seeds of what would later become a republic grounded in moral and spiritual truth. Their vision was carried forward by the Puritans, who established colonies with the express purpose of glorifying God and spreading His Word. These early settlers believed that they were called to create a society that would be a model for the rest of the world, a place where biblical principles would be lived out in every aspect of life.

In the book "Worldly Saints, The Puritans as They Really Were" by Leland Ryken, the Puritans are portrayed as a group of deeply religious and principled individuals who sought to bring every aspect of their lives into conformity with the teachings of the Bible. Contrary to their modern day reputation as strict, joyless, and repressive people, Ryken illustrates that the Puritans were actually much more complex and multifaceted. They were not only concerned with religious reform but also with cultivating a culture that honored God in all areas of life, from the church and family to work and politics.

The Puritans believed that their mission was to purify the church of England from its remaining catholic practices and bring about a more genuine form of christian worship. They viewed themselves as a chosen people on a divine mission to build a "city upon a hill" , a model christian society that would inspire reform across the world. They emphasized personal holiness, and the idea that all of life, even mundane tasks, should be carried out for the glory of God. The concept of the "covenant" was central to their thinking. They believed that God had made a covenant with them, and in turn, they were to live in obedience to His commandments to uphold their end of the relationship.

Ryken notes that the Puritans were known for their work ethic, a characteristic that stemmed from their belief that every job, no matter how small, had spiritual significance. To the Puritans labor was not a necessary evil but a calling from God, and success in work was a sign of divine favor. They also valued education, seeing it as crucial for understanding the Bible and living a godly life. As a result, they established schools and colleges, including Harvard, to train future generations in both religious and secular knowledge.

In "The Puritan Dilemma, The Story of John Winthrop" by Edmund Morgan, the Puritans' commitment to establishing a godly society is explored through the life of John Winthrop, one of their key leaders. Morgan explains that the Puritans faced the constant tension of living in the world but not being of it. They wanted to build a society based on christian principles while grappling with the reality of human sin and imperfection. This led to what Morgan describes as "the Puritan dilemma", the challenge of balancing their high ideals with the practicalities of life in the New World.

Winthrop and other Puritan leaders believed that the colony they were founding in Massachusetts was not just a political experiment but a divine mission. They viewed America as a new promised land where they could build a righteous society free from the corruption they saw in England. However, this also meant they had to enforce strict moral codes to maintain the purity of the community. Failure to live up to these standards was seen as a failure to uphold their covenant with God, and the Puritans were not afraid to impose harsh discipline on those who strayed from their ideals.

Both Ryken and Morgan show that the Puritans were far more than just a group of religious extremists. They were visionaries who sought to create a society that reflected their deepest religious convictions, and while they were not without their flaws, their influence on American culture, politics, and religion remains profound. Their legacy can be seen in the emphasis on hard work, education, and community that continues to shape American society to this day.

The founding fathers who were mostly devout christians, recognized the importance of these principles. They understood that the success of the American experiment depended on a moral and virtuous citizenry. John Adams famously remarked, "our constitution was made only for a moral and religious people. It is wholly inadequate to the government of any other." This wasn't just a throwaway line, it was a recognition of the truth that freedom and morality are inextricably linked. Without a moral foundation, freedom devolves into chaos. And for Adams and many of the other founders, that moral foundation could only be found in the judeo christian ethic.

This is not to suggest that the founders intended for America to be a theocracy. They clearly recognized the importance of religious freedom. But they also understood that a nation without a moral compass, guided by biblical truth, would eventually lose its way. The tension between freedom and morality has always been central to the American experience, and it's a tension that continues to shape our national identity to this day.

But somewhere along the way we lost sight of this truth. The covenant that the Pilgrims made with God has been breeched, and dismissed as irrelevant to our modern secular age. The idea that America was founded on biblical principles is often met with skepticism or outright hostility. In our public schools and universities, the story of America's christian roots has been rewritten, reduced to a footnote in the broader narrative of colonial exploitation and oppression.

And yet the evidence of our nation's biblical foundation is all around us. It's written into our founding documents, enshrined in our national symbols, and echoed in the speeches and writings of countless leaders throughout our history. George Washington, in his first inaugural address, made it clear that the success of the new republic depended on God's continued favor. He warned that we could not expect the "smiles of heaven", if we ignored the moral and spiritual principles that had brought us to that point.

In the book "Washington, A Life" by Ron Chernow, George Washington is depicted as a man of profound character, whose personal virtues played a pivotal role in shaping the early identity of the United States. Chernow portrays Washington as a figure whose sense of duty, moral fortitude, and commitment to the cause of liberty were unmatched among the founding fathers. Though often described as a stoic and reserved man, Washington was deeply reflective and his leadership was rooted in a desire to serve the greater good rather than seek personal glory.

Chernow illustrates how Washington's early experiences, from his time as a young surveyor in the wilderness to his leadership during the French and Indian war, honed his leadership abilities and sense of resilience. Washington's military career was marked by both triumphs and setbacks, but it was his ability to learn from failure and maintain an unshakable resolve that set him apart. By the time of the American revolution, Washington had earned a reputation as a man who could be trusted to lead with integrity and fairness, even in the most dire of circumstances.

Chernow emphasizes that one of Washington's defining characteristics was his humility. Despite being offered the chance to become a king like figure after the Revolution, Washington rejected any form of monarchical power, insisting on the principles of republicanism and democracy. His voluntary relinquishing of power after two terms as president cemented his legacy as a leader who put the nation's interests above his own. This act of stepping down willingly was unprecedented and set an enduring precedent for peaceful transitions of power in America.

In "His Excellency, George Washington" by Joseph Ellis, Washington's character is further explored through his commitment to self discipline and moral uprightness. Ellis explains that Washington was acutely aware of his public image and worked tirelessly to embody the virtues of honor, honesty, and patriotism. He believed that his personal conduct would serve as a model for the new nation's leaders, and thus he held himself to the highest possible standards. While Washington was not without flaws, Ellis points to his struggles with temper and occasional bouts of self doubt, his ability to rise above personal weaknesses in service of the greater good was what made him extraordinary.

Ellis also delves into Washington's complex relationship with power. Although he commanded immense authority, both as a general and as the nation's first president, he was always wary of its corrupting influence. This is perhaps best exemplified by his decision to resign his commission as commander and chief of the Continental Army after the revolution, returning to his farm at Mount Vernon. In a world where leaders often clung to power, Washington's act of stepping down was a powerful statement of his belief in republican ideals.

Both Chernow and Ellis highlight Washington's ability to unify disparate factions, both during the war and in the early years of the republic. His leadership style was one of consensus building, and he often sought the counsel of others, even when he disagreed with them. Washington understood that the success of the new nation depended on the cooperation of its citizens and leaders, and his steady hand at the helm helped guide the fledgling country through its formative years.

In these books, George Washington is depicted as the quintessential statesman, a man whose character and actions were instrumental in the creation and survival of the United States. His legacy endures not only in the nation's founding documents but in the very ethos of American leadership, a commitment to service, honor, and the greater good.

But it wasn't just the founders who recognized the importance of maintaining our covenant with God. Throughout our history, there have been periods of spiritual renewal, times when the church reasserted its influence in public life, reminding the nation of its responsibilities before God. The great awakenings, for example, were periods of intense religious revival that reshaped the moral and spiritual landscape of America. These revivals, led by preachers like Jonathan Edwards and George Whitefield, brought millions of people back to a sense of moral and spiritual duty.

In the book "The Great Awakening, The Roots of Evangelical Christianity in Colonial America" by Thomas S. Kidd, the Great Awakenings are explored as pivotal religious movements that fundamentally reshaped the spiritual and social landscape of America. Kidd describes the First Great Awakening, which occurred in the 1730s and 1740s, as a series of revivals that spread throughout the American colonies, led by influential preachers such as Jonathan Edwards and George Whitefield. These revivals emphasized personal conversion, heartfelt repentance, and the need for individuals to experience a profound, transformative relationship with God.

Kidd explains that one of the defining characteristics of the First Great Awakening was its challenge to the traditional authority of established churches. The movement stressed that salvation was not mediated by clergy or church membership, but rather through a direct, personal relationship with God. This radical message appealed to many, especially those who felt alienated by the formalism and perceived spiritual deadness of the established denominations. The revivals spread rapidly, igniting passionate responses among colonists, leading to the formation of new denominations, and the splintering of old ones.

In "Revival and Revivalism, The Making and Marring of American Evangelicalism 1750-1858" by Iain H. Murray, the second great awakening is explored in detail. Murray explains that this second wave of religious fervor, which began in the late 18th century and continued through the early 19th century, had an even broader social impact than the first. It was characterized by large scale camp meetings, emotional preaching, and a renewed emphasis on personal salvation and moral reform. Leaders such as Charles Finney and Francis Asbury played key roles in this movement, which reached far into the American frontier and helped fuel the rapid expansion of evangelical Protestantism.

Murray points out that the second great awakening also sparked a number of important social reforms. As people experienced personal renewal and felt a call to live out their faith in practical ways, many became involved in causes such as the abolition of slavery, temperance, and women's rights. The Awakening helped to plant the seeds of the social reform movements that would later define much of 19th century America.

Both Kidd and Murray emphasize that the Great Awakenings were not merely religious phenomena but had far reaching consequences for American culture and politics. This spirit of individualism and moral responsibility laid the groundwork for future social and political movements, including the fight for civil rights and the expansion of democratic participation.

In "The Great Awakening, A History of the Revival of Religion in the Time of Edwards and Whitefield" by Joseph Tracy, the emotional intensity of the revivals is further explored. Tracy details the powerful sermons and dramatic conversions that were hallmarks of the first great awakening, particularly the preaching of George Whitefield, who drew enormous crowds wherever he spoke. Whitefield's impassioned style, along with his message that God's grace was available to all, regardless of social standing, inspired thousands to repent of their sins and dedicate their lives to Christ. The revival meetings were often marked by visible signs of emotional distress, as listeners wept, cried out, or fell to the ground under conviction of sin.

Tracy also highlights the long term effects of the great awakenings on American religious life. The revivals not only led to the formation of new denominations, such as the Baptists and Methodists, but also fostered a sense of religious pluralism and competition. Established churches were no longer the only authorities on matters of faith, and the rise of evangelicalism provided a vibrant, alternative expression of christianity that would continue to shape the religious landscape of America for centuries to come.

Together, these books provide a comprehensive understanding of the great awakenings as transformative moments in American history. They were not only periods of intense spiritual revival but also movements that influenced the social, political, and cultural trajectory of the nation. The emphasis on personal faith, moral responsibility, and social reform during these revivals left an indelible mark on the character of American evangelicalism and the broader American ethos.

Also, the civil rights movement, was deeply rooted in biblical principles. Leaders like Martin Luther King Jr. appealed not just to the Constitution but to the Bible in their calls for justice and equality. The church in this case, was at the forefront of shaping the nation's conscience, challenging America to live up to its founding ideals.

But today, the church has largely retreated from public life. We've allowed secular voices to dominate the conversation, and in doing so we've abandoned our role as moral guardians of the nation. The biblical principles that once guided our laws and institutions have been replaced by a shifting relativistic moral code. And the results are clear, a nation in moral freefall where the very freedoms we hold dear are under threat.

This chapter and this book is not just a reflection on where we've been, but a call to return to where we began. The Pilgrims understood that their journey to the new world wasn't just about survival, it was about establishing a covenant with God, a covenant that would shape the destiny of this nation. It's time for us to remember that covenant.

The time has come for the church to find its voice again. To speak out against the moral decay that is eroding the foundations of our nation. To call our leaders and ourselves back to the principles that made America great. We are at a crossroads and the future of our nation hangs in the balance. Will we continue down the path of moral decline, or will we return to the covenant that once made us a "city upon a hill"? The choice is ours but the consequences of silence are too great to ignore.

Let this chapter serve as a reminder of where we began, and as a challenge to reclaim the covenant that set America apart from the beginning. If we do not we risk losing the very freedoms that were secured through the blood, sweat, and prayers of those who came before us.

CHAPTER 2 :

Hyper Grace, Distorting The Gospel

The hyper grace movement has has several names including but not limited to, radical grace, free grace, grace revolution, grace only movement, and extreme grace, gained significant traction in recent years, particularly among christians seeking a more "liberating" and "non judgmental" form of spirituality. With names like, Joseph Prince, Andrew Farley, Creflo Dollar, Tullian Tchividjian, Paul Ellis, and Clark Whitten just to mention a few.

At its core, hyper grace emphasizes the all encompassing grace of God while minimizing, if not outright ignoring, the need for repentance, obedience, and holiness. On the surface, this teaching may appear attractive. It promises freedom from guilt, fear, and condemnation. However, beneath this allure lies a dangerous distortion of the Gospel.

The fundamental issue with hyper grace is not its emphasis on grace itself. God's grace is indeed the foundation of the christian faith, but the incomplete and often imbalanced nature of its message. Proponents of hyper grace preach that once a person is saved, there is no need to worry about sin or its consequences. As all sins past, present, and future have been forgiven. While it is true that Christ's sacrifice covers all sin, this teaching strips the believer of accountability, sanctification, and growth in personal holiness.

The grace of God as outlined in Scripture, is not a license to sin. Paul addresses this directly in Romans 6:1-2 when he says, "Shall we go on sinning so that grace may abound? God forbid! We are those who have died to sin, how can we live in it any longer?" Grace is transformative, It changes the believer's heart, urging them to pursue righteousness and reflect the holiness of God. In the hyper grace movement this transformation is often downplayed or neglected, and the result is a passive christianity that does not strive for the character and will of Christ.

In the book "Hyper Grace, Exposing the Dangers of the Modern Grace Message" by Dr. Michael Brown, the author thoroughly critiques the theological underpinnings of the hyper grace movement, pointing out how it distorts traditional christian teachings on grace, sin, and sanctification. Dr. Brown argues that while grace is a central aspect of christian salvation, the hyper grace movement takes the concept too far by minimizing or even ignoring the believer's responsibility for repentance and holy living. He explains that this movement teaches that once someone is saved by grace, they no longer need to worry about sin because God has already forgiven their past, present, and future transgressions.

Brown emphasizes that this theology can lead to a kind of spiritual complacency, where christians no longer feel a need to strive for personal holiness or obedience to God's commands. He cites numerous scriptural passages to counter the hyper grace message, particularly highlighting how the New Testament repeatedly calls believers to pursue righteousness, resist sin, and grow in their faith. According to Brown, the hyper grace movement creates a false sense of security, as it effectively nullifies the need for self examination and repentance, which are essential elements of a genuine christian life.

In "The Grace Controversy" by Joseph Prince, the author defends many aspects of the hyper grace message but also inadvertently reveals some of the weaknesses and concerns critics like Dr. Brown have raised. Prince asserts that grace is meant to set christians free from the fear of condemnation and give them assurance of their eternal salvation. However, many theologians including those who have critiqued his work, point out that this assurance can lead to moral laxity. If christians believe their future sins are already forgiven, they might not see the importance of resisting sin in their daily lives.

Dr. Brown responds to these points in his own work by emphasizing the necessity of living out one's faith through actions. He points out that Paul, in his letters to the early churches, repeatedly warned against using grace as a license for sin. Instead, grace is meant to empower believers to live in obedience to God's Word, not as a way to excuse ongoing sinful behavior. Brown explains that by removing the need for repentance and downplaying the importance of sanctification, the hyper grace movement strips the gospel of its transformative power.

In "Charis, God's Scandalous Grace for Us" by Preston Sprinkle, the concept of grace is explored more broadly, though Sprinkle takes a more balanced approach than many proponents of the hyper grace movement. While he passionately defends the idea that God's grace is boundless and scandalously free, he also acknowledges that grace leads to transformation and growth in Christlikeness. Unlike some hyper grace teachers, Sprinkle does not dismiss the importance of good works or ongoing repentance. His work thus serves as a bridge between the hyper grace message and more traditional christian views on the relationship between grace and sanctification.

Brown and other critics argue that hyper grace theology has particularly damaging effects on the modern church because it encourages passivity in the face of evil and moral decay. Brown writes extensively about how churches influenced by hyper grace tend to avoid speaking out on issues like abortion, and even personal morality, under the guise that grace covers all wrongs and that judgment should be avoided. In his view, this creates a church that is inward focused, unconcerned with the suffering in the world, and disengaged from the call to be a moral and prophetic voice in society.

Dr. Brown also warns that the hyper grace movement can leave believers unprepared for spiritual warfare, as it downplays the reality of sin and the ongoing battle against the flesh. By failing to emphasize the need for vigilance and self discipline, hyper grace theology can lead to spiritual apathy, leaving christians vulnerable to temptation and moral compromise. This is why Brown calls for a return to a more biblically balanced understanding of grace, one that fully embraces God's mercy and forgiveness but also recognizes the call to live a holy and righteous life.

In these books, we see a sharp contrast between traditional christian teachings on grace and the hyper grace movement. While proponents of hyper grace argue that their theology frees christians from guilt and condemnation, critics like Dr. Brown believe it fosters a shallow, incomplete understanding of discipleship, leading to spiritual stagnation and moral decay. As the hyper grace message continues to gain popularity, its critics call for a reawakening to the full gospel message, a message that includes both the free gift of grace and the call to live in obedient faith.

One of the most concerning aspects of hyper grace theology is the lack of conviction about sin. In the name of "not being judgmental," the movement frequently avoids any confrontation of sin, both on an individual and societal level. Hyper grace preachers rarely address issues like sexual immorality, greed, injustice, or the sanctity of life because doing so would make people feel uncomfortable or judged. In this worldview the only sin is to make someone feel convicted. As a result the church's prophetic voice is muted, unable to speak truth to power or to the culture at large.

The Bible calls the church to be salt and light in the world, Matthew 5:13-16, yet the hyper grace movement often fails to fulfill this mandate. By refusing to call out evil and address societal decay, it creates a church that is complicit in the moral decline of the nation. When sin is not confronted it grows like a cancer, leading to greater destruction in society. Hyper grace offers comfort without transformation, leaving the world unchanged and the church powerless.

Given its aversion to calling out sin, it's no surprise that the hyper grace movement is virtually silent in the face of the widespread cultural evil plaguing modern society. Whether it's the sexualization of children in schools, the sanctity of human life in the abortion debate, or the breakdown of the family unit, hyper grace churches rarely take a stand. Instead they preach a message of acceptance and tolerance, hoping to win over people with love while neglecting the biblical mandate to stand against evil, Ephesians 5:11.

The church is meant to be a beacon of truth and justice, confronting evil and promoting righteousness in every sphere of life. However, a church steeped in hyper grace theology is ill equipped to do so. Without a robust theology of sin and righteousness, there is no moral framework from which to challenge the culture. As a result, hyper grace churches often avoid involvement in critical social and political issues, leaving the battle for the soul of the nation to others.

The true grace of God is not passive, it is active and powerful. It not only saves us from our sins but also empowers us to live in victory over them. Biblical grace calls us to repentance and transformation. It pushes us to grow in righteousness and seek to align our lives with the will of God. In Titus 2:11-12, Paul writes, "For the grace of God has appeared that offers salvation to all people. It teaches us to say no to ungodliness and worldly passions, and to live self controlled, upright, and godly lives in this present age."

This is the grace the church must rediscover. A grace that saves, transforms, and empowers believers to stand up for righteousness in a world that desperately needs it. The church cannot afford to remain silent or passive in the face of evil. The hyper grace movement's refusal to engage in the moral and spiritual battles of our time has left a vacuum that must be filled with the truth of the Gospel.

True grace doesn't ignore sin, it confronts it. True grace doesn't tolerate evil, it stands against it. The church must reject the watered down message of hyper grace and return to the full Gospel, which includes both the grace that forgives and the truth that transforms. Only then can the church fulfill its calling as the salt and light of the world, standing boldly against the darkness and proclaiming the righteousness of God.

CHAPTER 3

Ignoring Evil : The Church's Silence In Nazi Germany

The German church's failure to stand up to Adolf Hitler had devastating consequences, not only for the Jews and other persecuted groups but also for the church itself. As the Nazi regime grew more powerful, the church found that its attempts to appease Hitler only led to greater restrictions on its freedom. Nazi ideology, which glorified the state and Adolf Hitler as a messianic figure, sought to undermine christian teachings that emphasized the authority of Christ and the intrinsic value of every human life.

By the time the church realized the full extent of Hitler's evil, it was too late. The Nazis had infiltrated every aspect of society, including the church itself, through the German christian movement, which sought to merge Nazi ideology with christianity. The cost of the church's silence was immense, millions of lives were lost in the Holocaust, and the moral authority of the church in Germany was forever tarnished.

The story of the German church's failure to oppose Hitler serves as a sobering reminder for the modern church. In today's world there are many forms of evil that the church is called to confront. Whether it be the destruction of the family, the disregard for human life, the persecution of christians abroad, or the moral relativism that pervades society. Yet much like the church in Nazi Germany, many christians today remain silent.

Just as the German church feared losing its influence and facing persecution, today's church often avoids controversial issues to protect its comfort or reputation. Whether it's the fear of being labeled intolerant, politically incorrect, or divisive, many church leaders shy away from addressing moral and social issues head on. This silence comes at a great cost. When the church fails to speak up, evil goes unchecked, and society drifts further into moral decay.

The church is called to be a voice for truth, even when it is unpopular or dangerous. In Matthew 5:13-16, Jesus refers to His followers as the salt of the earth and the light of the world. Salt preserves what is good and prevents decay, while light exposes darkness. The church must take seriously its responsibility to fulfill this role, or else it will lose its effectiveness, much like the German church did during the rise of Nazism.

The lessons from Nazi Germany call christians to courage and conviction. If the church had stood up to Hitler early on, it might have prevented much if not all of the devastation that followed. While it is impossible to change the past, the church today can learn from these mistakes and refuse to let history repeat itself. Believers are called to be bold in the face of evil, to defend the oppressed, and to speak out against injustice, even at personal cost.

One of the primary reasons the German church failed to oppose Hitler was its disunity. There were divisions within the church between protestants and catholics, between conservative and liberal theologians, and even within the protestant church itself. There were those who supported Hitler and those who opposed him. This lack of unity weakened the church's ability to present a united front against evil.

In today's church similar divisions exist, whether along denominational, theological, or political lines. These divisions can distract the church from its higher calling to be a force for righteousness in the world. It is imperative that christians put aside lesser differences to unite in opposition to the evil that threatens society. Whether it's the issue of abortion, the erosion of religious freedom, or the spread of secularism, the church must stand together in defense of biblical truth.

The Barmen Declaration

The Barmen Declaration was a theological statement formulated in May 1934 by a group of German church leaders. It was primarily led by Karl Barth, in response to the rise of national socialism, and the increasing influence of the Nazi ideology on the protestant churches in Germany. The declaration was adopted by the confessing church, a movement within the German protestant church that opposed the Nazis' attempt to align christianity with its totalitarian, racist, and nationalist ideology.

After Adolf Hitler came to power in 1933, the Nazi regime sought to unify all aspects of German society, including the churches, under its control. The German evangelical church, a protestant body, was particularly targeted for "coordination", Gleichschaltung, a process that aimed to align it with Nazi policies. The so called, "German Christians", Deutsche Christen, a pro Nazi faction within the church, supported the regime's efforts to infuse christianity with Nazi ideology, including anti semitism and the Führer principle, which promoted loyalty to Hitler as an expression of christian faith.

Many church leaders however, recognized that the Nazi ideology was fundamentally incompatible with biblical christianity. The Barmen Declaration was their response, affirming the authority of scripture and the centrality of Christ, while rejecting the subordination of the church to any earthly power, including the state.

The declaration consists of six theses, each rejecting specific Nazi influences on the church and affirming core Christian beliefs. Here are some key points from the document.

Christ as the Sole Head of the Church. The declaration insists that Jesus Christ is the one and only Word of God, through whom humanity receives salvation. No other authority, whether political or ideological, could replace Christ's lordship over the church. This was a direct rejection of the Nazi attempt to elevate Hitler to a quasi divine status within the church.

"Jesus Christ, as He is attested to us in Holy Scripture, is the one Word of God which we have to hear and which we have to trust and obey in life and in death."

The Barmen Declaration rejects any attempt to blend the message of the Gospel with political ideologies. The document emphasizes that the church's message is derived from scripture, not from any earthly ruler or authority.

The Barmen Declaration rejects the idea that the state has any authority over the internal affairs of the church or its proclamation of the Gospel. This was a response to Nazi efforts to control church governance and teachings.

"We reject the false idea that the church should look to other events, powers, historical figures, or so called truths, alongside or apart from the Word of God, as sources of divine revelation."

"The christian church is the community of brethren in which in word and sacrament, through the Holy Spirit, Jesus Christ acts presently as the Lord in the world. We reject the false doctrine, as though the Church were permitted to abandon the form of its message and order to its own pleasure or to changes in prevailing ideological and political convictions."

The Barmen Declaration was a courageous act of defiance against the Nazi regime and a profound statement of christian integrity. By affirming the authority of Christ over all worldly powers, the confessing church drew a clear line between the true gospel and the ideologically corrupted version promoted by the Nazis. The declaration inspired resistance among many christians, though it also led to persecution. Many leaders of the confessing church, including Martin Niemöller and Dietrich Bonhoeffer, were arrested, and some, like Bonhoeffer, were eventually executed.

Bonhoeffer believed that the church's witness would be proven not by words alone but by actions. By standing with the oppressed, even if it meant suffering the consequences.

In his sermons and writings, he continued to call on christians to resist the Nazi regime and to act on their faith, even at great personal cost. Bonhoeffer was deeply critical of christians who claimed that they could remain neutral, that the church's only role was to preach the gospel without confronting the political realities of the day. To him, this was a gross misunderstanding of the gospel. He wrote,

 "Silence in the face of evil is itself evil, God will not hold us guiltless. Not to speak is to speak. Not to act is to act."

As Hitler's grip on Germany tightened, Bonhoeffer's warnings became even more urgent. In his book "The Cost of Discipleship," published in 1937, he argued that christianity required radical obedience to Christ, obedience that demanded action in the face of injustice. He contrasted "cheap grace" with "costly grace." Cheap grace, he said, was the preaching of forgiveness without requiring repentance, baptism without church discipline, and communion without confession. Costly grace, on the other hand, was grace that called a man to follow Christ even to death.

Bonhoeffer's theology was not just theoretical, it was lived out in his resistance to the Nazi regime. As the persecution of Jews intensified, Bonhoeffer became involved in the Abwehr, a German military intelligence organization that was secretly plotting to overthrow Hitler. While serving as a double agent, Bonhoeffer helped smuggle Jews out of Germany and worked with resistance groups, risking his life for what he knew was right.

Despite Bonhoeffer's tireless efforts, the church as a whole remained largely complicit or passive in the face of Nazi atrocities. Many church leaders believed that their primary duty was to maintain order and preserve their institutions, rather than confront the regime. Even those who opposed the Nazis often felt powerless or unwilling to act, fearing the loss of their positions or the destruction of their churches.

In 1943, as the war turned against Germany, Bonhoeffer was arrested by the Gestapo. He was imprisoned for nearly two years, during which time he continued to write and encourage those around him to resist evil. Even in prison, Bonhoeffer maintained his unshakeable faith that the church had a role to play in confronting injustice. He continued to call on the church to confess its guilt for failing to protect the Jews and for its complicity in the regime's crimes.

In April 1945, just weeks before the end of the war, Bonhoeffer was executed by hanging at the Flossenbürg concentration camp. His death came just days before American forces liberated the camp. Bonhoeffer's final words, as recorded by a fellow prisoner, were, "This is the end for me, the beginning of life."

Bonhoeffer's martyrdom stands as a testament to his unwavering commitment to the Gospel and his belief that the church must not only preach the Word but also live it out in the face of injustice, no matter the cost. He had spent his life trying to awaken the church to its moral responsibility, but in the end, it was his own life that became the ultimate witness.

Bonhoeffer's life and legacy serve as a stark reminder of the church's responsibility to stand up against evil. He saw the storm coming long before many of his peers and tried to warn them, but the institutional church, gripped by fear, nationalism, and complicity, failed to heed his call.

His story is one of hope, faith, and conviction, but it is also a warning of what happens when the church remains silent in the face of evil. In the end, Bonhoeffer's voice echoes through history as a challenge to the modern church to never again allow evil to go unchecked, to speak out, to act, and to follow Christ, no matter the cost.

In the book Ordinary Men, Christopher Browning provides an in depth and chilling look at the men of Reserve Police Battalion 101, a group of roughly 500 middle aged, working class men from Hamburg who were neither elite soldiers nor dedicated Nazis. These men, many of whom had little prior military training and came from ordinary backgrounds, truck drivers, dockworkers, and salesmen, found themselves tasked with some of the most brutal aspects of Hitler's final solution in Nazi occupied Poland. Their story, as told by Browning, is a powerful illustration of how average individuals can be transformed into perpetrators of unspeakable atrocities through the pressures of obedience, authority, and conformity.

One of the key events in the book revolves around the battalion's first massacre in the small village of Józefów on July 13, 1942. It was here that these "ordinary" men were first exposed to the task of systematically murdering Jewish civilians. Early in the morning, the battalion's commander, Major Wilhelm Trapp, a career officer and a veteran of World War I, gathered his men for an ominous briefing. Visibly emotional and distraught, Trapp explained that their assignment was to round up the Jews in Józefów and execute those who were deemed unfit for work primarily the elderly, women, and children.

Trapp's demeanor was striking. He was openly shaken, apologetic even, expressing to his men that this was not an easy task. He acknowledged that many of them might find it hard to carry out such an order, and in a surprising move, he offered them a choice, any man who did not feel up to the task of shooting civilians could step forward and be excused from the mission without punishment. This rare gesture, which broke from the strict obedience expected in the Nazi military, presented the men with a moral crossroads. It was an opportunity to refuse participation in mass murder, a decision that could potentially allow them to avoid the weight of guilt that would come from killing innocent people.

Despite this offer, only about a dozen men roughly ten percent of the battalion stepped forward. The vast majority remained silent, unwilling or unable to take this out. For most, the pressure to conform, the desire to avoid being seen as cowardly or disloyal, and the fear of social ostracism from their comrades were powerful forces that outweighed their personal moral objections. Some later admitted that they were unsure what stepping forward would truly mean, fearing repercussions or embarrassment in front of their peers. Others rationalized their compliance by convincing themselves that if they didn't do it, someone else would.

What followed was one of the most horrifying episodes in the battalion's history. The men were divided into groups and led into the village. As they rounded up the Jewish inhabitants, separating those who were fit for work from those who were to be executed, the gravity of the task began to sink in. The executions took place in a nearby forest, where the victims were brought in groups and shot one by one. Many of the men, who had never before fired a gun in anger or been involved in violence, found themselves facing terrified civilians, women clutching their children, elderly men unable to walk, young children barely able to comprehend what was happening.

The psychological toll of that first massacre was immense. Several of the men, overwhelmed by the horror of what they were doing, broke down emotionally. Some vomited, others wept openly, and a few became so distraught that they asked to be reassigned to less direct roles. Despite this, the killing continued throughout the day. By the end of the massacre, over 1,500 Jewish men, women, and children lay dead in the forest, executed by these ordinary policemen.

For many of the men in the battalion, the massacre at Józefów marked a turning point. In the days and weeks that followed, Browning describes how they dealt with the trauma of their actions in different ways. Some continued to express deep discomfort, but most found ways to rationalize their participation. They told themselves that they were following orders, that this was part of the war effort, or that their individual refusal wouldn't have made a difference since the killings would have happened with or without them. Over time, the men became increasingly desensitized to the violence.

As the battalion continued to carry out its gruesome work across other villages and ghettos in Poland, what had initially been shocking and disturbing became routine. The men's initial reluctance gave way to an acceptance of their role in the Holocaust. They learned to compartmentalize the horror, separating their actions as "soldiers" from their personal lives. Some even took pride in their efficiency, becoming more adept at carrying out mass shootings and rounding up Jews for deportation to death camps. What was once unimaginable became a part of their daily lives.

Browning's exploration of the psychology behind this transformation is a central theme in Ordinary Men. He argues that the men of reserve police battalion 101 were not fanatical ideologues or hardened killers by nature. Rather, they were average men who were shaped by their circumstances by the pressures of authority, the dynamics of the group, and the fear of standing out. The decision not to step forward at Józefów was not just about following orders, it was about the powerful human desire to conform, to avoid conflict with peers, and to preserve one's own sense of normalcy in an abnormal situation.

One of the most poignant aspects of the story is that, throughout their deployment, the men of battalion 101 were never under threat of punishment for refusing to participate in the killings. In fact, those who did refuse were often reassigned to other duties without facing any formal reprimand. This fact underscores the moral weight of their choices. Despite not being coerced, the vast majority chose to follow orders. Browning highlights this as a chilling reminder of how ordinary individuals can be drawn into evil, not through coercion or fanaticism, but through compliance and a lack of moral resistance.

The story of reserve police battalion 101 is a powerful cautionary tale for christians today. Just as these "ordinary men" allowed themselves to become agents of genocide through their passivity and willingness to obey immoral orders, the church today faces its own moral test. The story echoes the broader message of this book, that when evil arises, silence and passivity are not neutral choices. They are, in fact, forms of complicity.

In the context of Nazi Germany, the christian church, which had the numbers and the moral authority to resist, largely remained silent or complicit in the face of the Holocaust. The story of battalion 101 serves as a stark reminder of the dangers of failing to stand up against injustice, no matter the cost. It also illustrates how easily people can rationalize their inaction, telling themselves that their refusal to participate won't change the outcome.

But the lesson from Ordinary Men is clear, when faced with moral evil, every individual, and by extension, every institution including the church has a choice to make. The men of battalion 101, like many christians in Nazi Germany, chose the path of least resistance. They allowed themselves to become instruments of horror because they didn't have the moral courage to refuse. Today, the church faces its own set of moral challenges. The question is whether it will stand up and speak out against the evils of our time, or whether it will follow the path of the "ordinary men" of reserve police battalion 101 and choose silence, conformity, and complicity.

The chilling transformation of these ordinary men serves as a powerful reminder that evil often thrives not through the actions of a few fanatics, but through the compliance of the many who are unwilling to resist. It is a lesson that the church must heed if it is to avoid repeating the mistakes of the past.

The Manhattan Declaration

A call of christian conscience was issued in November 2009 by a coalition of christian leaders from various denominations. Evangelical, catholic, and orthodox sought to unite in defense of traditional christian values amidst growing cultural and legal challenges in the United States. The declaration emphasizes the importance of protecting life, upholding the biblical definition of marriage, and defending religious freedom.

The Manhattan Declaration was drafted by Robert P. George, a Catholic legal scholar from Princeton University, along with Evangelical leaders Chuck Colson and Timothy George. It was released during a time when cultural and political shifts in the U.S. were increasingly challenging christian teachings on life, marriage, and religious liberty.

The document was prompted by several significant societal changes, including the legalization and growing societal acceptance of abortion and euthanasia. And the push for same sex marriage and the redefinition of marriage away from its traditional biblical understanding.

Growing concerns about the erosion of religious liberty, particularly with regard to christian institutions being pressured to conform to secular values, such as providing services that violate their beliefs, like providing contraception or performing abortions.

The Manhattan Declaration was a rallying cry for christians to stand firm in their convictions on these foundational moral issues, even if it meant civil disobedience.

The declaration focuses on three main areas of concern for christians in the public square.

The declaration affirms the sacredness of every human life, from conception to natural death. It strongly opposes abortion, euthanasia, and any other practices that undermine the value of human life. The signatories pledge to work toward the legal protection of life and to resist any laws or policies that promote the culture of death.

"Because the sanctity of human life is so inviolable, we will not comply with any edict that compels us to participate in, or facilitate, an abortion, embryo destructive research, assisted suicide, euthanasia, or any other act that deliberately takes innocent human life."

 The Manhattan Declaration upholds the traditional christian understanding of marriage as a covenantal union between one man and one woman. It opposes the redefinition of marriage to include same sex couples, arguing that such redefinitions undermine the biblical and natural law foundations of society.

"We acknowledge that there are those who do not share our understanding of marriage and sexuality, and we do not seek to demean them or their moral views. But we cannot stand idly by while those who adhere to these principles are forced to choose between being faithful to their consciences or being forced to violate their deeply held beliefs."

The declaration stresses the importance of religious liberty as a fundamental human right, given by God, not granted by the state. It warns against the increasing pressure on christians to conform to secular ideologies, particularly in areas of life and marriage, and pledges civil disobedience where necessary to uphold religious freedom.

"We will not comply with any edict that violates our God given right to follow our consciences."

The Manhattan Declaration serves as a bold statement of christian conviction in the face of growing secularism and legal challenges. It was signed by over 150 prominent christian leaders from various denominations and has since been supported by hundreds of thousands of individuals.

The declaration is significant because it represents a united front among diverse christian traditions on key moral issues. It also underscores the belief that christians must be prepared to engage in civil disobedience if necessary to defend their moral convictions, particularly when it comes to issues of life, marriage, and religious liberty.

In the context of Nazi Germany and the church's response to totalitarianism, the Manhattan Declaration echoes the spirit of the Barmen Declaration by calling christians to resist cultural and political forces that compromise core biblical values. Both documents call for a faithful, uncompromising stand against tyranny, whether it comes in the form of Nazi ideology or modern secularism.

The church's silence in Nazi Germany serves as a cautionary tale for believers today. When the church fails to speak out against evil, it not only fails to fulfill its biblical mandate, but it also becomes complicit in the destruction that follows. Christians must resist the temptation to compromise or remain silent in the face of moral challenges. Instead, the church must stand boldly for truth, justice, and righteousness, uniting to confront the evils of the present day just as it should have confronted the evil of Hitler's regime.

In the end, the church is not called to preserve its own comfort or safety, but to be a prophetic voice in the world, speaking truth to power and standing up for what is right, regardless of the cost. If the church fails to do so, history warns us that the consequences can be dire.

CHAPTER 4 :

The Sexualization Of Children, Where Is The Church?

Let's take a moment to confront the elephant in the room. It's not as if the church doesn't see what's happening. It's not that the christians in this country are blind to the decay, the corruption, the moral bankruptcy spreading like wildfire. No, the issue isn't ignorance, it's indifference. We know. We see it. We just don't care enough to act.

Let's be honest for a second. How many times have we heard the phrase, "Well, the world's going to hell anyway, so what can we do?" It's like we've accepted defeat before even putting on our armor. We have entire congregations shrugging their shoulders while the culture spirals into madness. I've even heard some say, "This world is passing away, so we shouldn't get involved in politics or try to change the culture." Really? That's your excuse?

Imagine if the early christians had that attitude. "Well, Rome is going to collapse anyway, so why bother preaching the Gospel? Why bother standing up for righteousness?" If they thought like that, there would be no church today. No one would've heard the Gospel. But the early christians didn't sit back and wait for the apocalypse, they went into the streets, the arenas, the public squares, risking their lives, because they knew that God's truth needed to be spoken. They weren't waiting for the rapture to escape their problems. They were busy fighting for the kingdom, knowing that God had placed them in their time and place for a reason.

And here we are, in one of the most critical moments in history, and what are we doing? Posting Bible verses on Facebook and hoping someone else will "make a difference." Well, I hate to break it to you, but the Bible didn't tell us to stay in our safe little christian bubble. It told us to go into the world and make disciples. It told us to shine the light in the darkness, not sit around and wait for someone else to do it.

But instead, we have entire churches that have become sanctuaries of silence. Sanctuaries of avoidance. They'd rather stay comfortable, stay neutral, stay silent, because speaking out might offend someone. Oh no, we wouldn't want to offend anyone with the truth, would we? Meanwhile, the world is burning down around us, and we're sitting on our hands, hoping it will just go away. Spoiler alert, it won't !

And you know what the craziest part is? Most of the church doesn't even realize how deep the rot goes. It's like we're standing in the middle of a sinking ship, and everyone's busy rearranging the deck chairs. "Let's focus on having a great worship experience this Sunday," they say, while the culture drowns in confusion and evil. We're losing our country, but hey, at least the worship music was good, right?

This isn't about politics. It's not about left or right. It's about righteousness. It's about God's people standing up for what's right, no matter what the cost. But somehow, we've convinced ourselves that it's okay to stay out of the fight. We tell ourselves that it's someone else's problem. We say, "God is in control," as if that means we can just sit back and watch everything fall apart, without lifting a finger to do anything about it.

Here's the truth. Yes, God is in control, but He also commands His people to act. He commands us to be the salt of the earth, to be the light of the world. Salt isn't passive. Salt prevents decay. Light isn't passive either, it pierces the darkness. But if the salt loses its saltiness, it's worthless. And if the light is hidden, it's useless.

We've become a generation of hidden lights. And because of that, the darkness is winning. More unborn babies are being murdered, more children are being indoctrinated with evil ideologies, more families are being torn apart. And yet, the church stays silent, feeling perfectly justified in its inaction.

But here's the thing, God doesn't stay silent. History shows us that when His people refuse to stand up for what's right, God will raise up someone else. He'll find another way. But do we really want to be the generation that let the country fall apart because we couldn't be bothered to speak up? Do we want to be remembered as the christians who stood by and did nothing while evil ran rampant?

Let me tell you something sobering, one day, we'll stand before God, and He's not going to ask how good we were at avoiding conflict. He's going to ask what we did with the truth He gave us. And if all we have to show for ourselves is a collection of Instagram posts and a handful of vague prayers, we're going to be in for a rude awakening.

The power is in our hands. Not just the power of words, but the power to change the course of history. If we speak out, if we stand up for righteousness, God will back us up with His power, greater than any government, greater than any institution, greater than any evil we face. But if we stay silent? Well, we've already seen what happens when the church stays silent. Societies crumble and nations fall. And the blood is on our hands.

So, it's time to wake up. It's time to stop playing church and start being the church. The time for silence is over. We've been given a voice, let's use it before it's too late.

In today's world, children are increasingly being exposed to sexually explicit content at younger and younger ages, especially in public schools.

From graphic sex education curriculums to the normalization of gender ideology, there is an alarming trend towards the sexualization of children. What's even more concerning is the relative silence from the church on this issue. While this trend advances many churches have remained quiet, afraid to confront the cultural forces pushing these agendas.

This chapter explores the grave issue of the sexualization of children in our public schools. Why it's happening, and how the church's lack of action is allowing this dangerous movement to gain ground. More importantly it issues a call for christians to wake up and take a stand against the corruption of young minds.

Sexualized content in public schools is no longer a fringe issue. Across the country parents are discovering that their children are being taught material that is not only inappropriate but also harmful. In many cases, these lessons go far beyond the basics of reproduction, entering into areas of sexual orientation, gender identity, and explicit descriptions of sexual activity, at shockingly young ages.

 These programs often include discussions on gender fluidity, alternative sexual lifestyles, and even techniques of contraception and sexual experimentation. While the stated goal of these programs is to promote inclusivity and safe practices. The reality is that they want to corrupt the minds of your children.

In Liz Wheeler's book Hide Your Children, one of the most compelling stories she shares is about a mother named Sarah, who found herself in a battle she never expected to fight, protecting her children from radical ideologies being pushed in their school. Sarah's story is a powerful illustration of how ordinary parents can be thrust into the heart of the culture wars, and how their courage and persistence can make a difference.

Sarah, a devout christian, lived in a suburban community where she assumed the local public schools would provide a safe and healthy environment for her children. For years, she trusted the school system, believing that her children were receiving a well rounded education that aligned with the family's values. But everything changed when her youngest child, Emma, came home one day deeply confused after a lesson on gender identity.

In the class, the teacher introduced the idea that gender is not a biological reality, but rather a "fluid concept" that children could choose for themselves. Emma, only nine years old, was taught that she could decide whether she was a girl, a boy, or something else. The lesson wasn't just a passing mention, it was part of a broader curriculum designed to promote gender ideology, with teachers actively encouraging children to explore different gender identities and pronouns.

Sarah was horrified. She had never been informed that this kind of material would be taught, and she felt that her rights as a parent were being completely undermined. She immediately contacted the school, asking for clarification and requesting that her child be exempt from these lessons. The school's response was dismissive. They told her that the curriculum was in place to "create an inclusive environment" and that opting out was not an option. They assured her that this was the direction education was headed, and there was nothing she could do to change it.

Refusing to accept this, Sarah decided to take matters into her own hands. She began to research more about what was happening in schools across the country and discovered that the gender ideology being pushed in her daughter's classroom was part of a much larger agenda, one that aimed to reshape children's understanding of family, morality, and identity. She joined forces with other concerned parents in her community, and together they started attending school board meetings, demanding transparency and accountability from the school district.

At these meetings, Sarah and the other parents were met with hostility. The school board dismissed their concerns as "intolerant" and accused them of trying to stifle progress. Sarah was even labeled a "bigot" for questioning the curriculum. But she refused to back down. With the help of organizations like Moms for Liberty, Sarah and her group began organizing rallies and petitioning the school district to remove the radical gender curriculum. They gathered signatures from hundreds of parents who felt similarly betrayed by the schools they once trusted.

As the movement gained traction, the story caught the attention of local media. News outlets began covering the controversy, and soon parents across the state were joining the fight. The pushback was fierce, but so was the resistance from school officials and activists who were determined to keep the curriculum in place. The school district, under pressure from the media and public outcry, finally agreed to hold an open forum where parents could voice their concerns.

At the forum, Sarah delivered a powerful speech. She spoke passionately about her love for her children and her conviction that parents, not schools, should be the ones to teach children about sensitive issues like gender and sexuality. She argued that the school's curriculum was not only inappropriate for young children but also in direct opposition to the values she and many other parents were trying to instill at home. Her words struck a chord with many in the audience, and more parents began to speak out.

In the months that followed, Sarah's activism grew. She and other parents continued to put pressure on the school board, filing complaints and organizing protests. Their persistence paid off when the school district finally agreed to scale back the controversial curriculum and implement an opt out policy for parents who did not want their children exposed to certain lessons. It was a small victory, but a significant one, and it demonstrated the power of parents who were willing to stand up for their beliefs.

Sarah's story, as shared by Liz Wheeler, is a testament to the fact that ordinary people can make a difference when they refuse to stay silent. Sarah didn't set out to become an activist, but when her child's innocence was threatened, she was compelled to act. Her courage inspired other parents to do the same, and together, they were able to push back against a powerful agenda that sought to undermine parental rights and impose radical ideas on children.

Just as Sarah refused to allow her daughter to be indoctrinated, christians must also take a stand against the forces seeking to erode the values that have long defined our faith, our families, and our nation. Sarah's story is a call to action for parents, churches, and communities to wake up, get involved, and fight back against the cultural forces threatening our children's future.

In many cases, the teaching of gender ideology is done under the guise of inclusivity, but what it actually does is sow confusion and create a false narrative that goes against biological and biblical truth. The church should be at the forefront of challenging this ideology, yet too often it remains on the sidelines, avoiding the topic altogether for fear of being labeled intolerant or unloving.

In the book Standing Up to Goliath by Rebecca Friedrichs, the author delivers a powerful and detailed exposé on the public school system's deep entanglement with teachers' unions, particularly highlighting how these unions have played a significant role in the sexualization of children and pushing harmful agendas onto students. Friedrichs, a former public school teacher who became an outspoken advocate for educational reform, recounts her personal experiences with the toxic influence of the unions and their agenda. Showing how these groups prioritize political power over the well being of children and their education.

Friedrichs explains that one of the most disturbing aspects of the unions' influence is their promotion of hypersexualized content in classrooms. She describes how the unions consistently push for sex education programs that are not age appropriate and that go far beyond simply teaching the biological facts of life. Instead, they advocate for curriculums that introduce sexual content to children at increasingly younger ages, promoting ideologies that encourage sexual experimentation, gender confusion, and even the normalization of pornography. Friedrichs argues that these programs are designed not to educate children, but to indoctrinate them into a radical worldview that strips away innocence and undermines the authority of parents.

Throughout the book, Friedrichs details how teachers who speak out against these curriculums or voice concerns about the well being of their students are often silenced or bullied by the unions. She describes cases where teachers were forced to teach material they knew was harmful or developmentally inappropriate for their students. Simply because the unions had negotiated the curriculums into contracts and made them mandatory. Those who refused to comply were ostracized or even threatened with job loss.

Friedrichs goes further, exposing the unions' broader political agenda, which extends far beyond the classroom. She explains how the unions pour millions of dollars into political campaigns and lobby for policies that have little to do with education but everything to do with advancing their progressive social agenda. These policies, she argues, are contributing to the breakdown of the traditional family, the erosion of parental rights, and the sexualization of children. Friedrichs asserts that the unions do not care about the long term consequences of their actions, as their primary goal is to maintain political power and control over the education system.

Moreover, Friedrichs highlights how the unions have systematically removed parents from the decision making process. Often framing them as adversaries rather than partners in their children's education. The unions push policies that limit parental involvement and promote the idea that the state knows better than parents when it comes to raising and educating children. This, she argues is a direct assault on the foundational role of the family and a key factor in the moral and academic decline seen in public schools across the country.

In Standing Up to Goliath, Friedrichs also delves into the unions' broader cultural impact, particularly their support for movements and policies that undermine judeo christian values and promote a secular, relativistic worldview. She connects the dots between the sexualization of children, the erosion of parental authority, and the unions' larger goal of transforming society to fit their radical, progressive ideology. Friedrichs argues that these unions are not merely fighting for teachers' rights or better pay but are leading a cultural revolution that is deeply harmful to the next generation.

Friedrichs' book is a clarion call to parents, teachers, and citizens to wake up to the reality of what is happening in America's public schools. She calls for parents to reclaim their authority, to demand transparency in what their children are being taught, and to push back against the unions that are corrupting the educational system. Friedrichs makes it clear that the fight is not just about education, but about the future of the nation itself, and the souls of the children who are being shaped by these powerful and often sinister forces.

So, why isn't the church speaking out against this alarming trend? There are several reasons for this silence, and none of them are justifiable given the biblical mandate to protect the most vulnerable among us. For one, many churches have bought into the idea that engaging in cultural battles is "political" and therefore not within the church's purview. Others may fear losing members or being criticized as hateful or bigoted for opposing the dominant cultural narrative.

There is also a growing movement within some christian circles that advocates for a softer, less confrontational approach to moral issues. This "love and acceptance" model often leads churches to avoid tough topics altogether, preferring to focus on personal spiritual growth rather than societal transformation. While love and grace are essential components of the christian faith, they must never be divorced from truth. Ignoring or downplaying sin, especially when it harms the innocent, is not loving, it is a failure of moral responsibility.

The consequences of the church's silence on the sexualization of children are profound. When the church fails to take a stand, it leaves a moral vacuum that allows secular and progressive agendas to flourish. Children are left vulnerable to ideologies that distort their understanding of identity, sexuality, and morality, and the societal damage caused by this can be devastating.

As a result, many parents feel isolated and powerless in the face of an education system that seems more interested in social engineering than in teaching academics. Without the church's support and leadership, christian parents are left to fight these battles on their own, often without the necessary resources or backing to make meaningful change. The church must be the moral voice that helps equip parents to protect their children from these harmful influences.

Moreover, inaction on this issue perpetuates the idea that the church is irrelevant to modern societal concerns. When christians refuse to address what is happening in schools, they send the message that these issues are unimportant, further alienating those who look to the church for guidance and truth.

The Bible is clear about the importance of protecting children. Jesus Himself gave stern warnings about causing little ones to stumble, Matthew 18:6. Throughout Scripture, children are seen as a blessing from God, and there is a high calling placed on parents and the community of believers to nurture, protect, and teach them in the ways of the Lord, Deuteronomy 6:6-7.

Allowing children to be exposed to sexual content and confusing ideologies that undermine their identity is a direct violation of this biblical mandate. The church cannot stand idly by while children's innocence is stolen, their minds are corrupted, and their understanding of truth is warped. The church is called to be a defender of the vulnerable, and there are few groups more vulnerable than young children.

The church must first recognize that the sexualization of children is not just a political or social issue, it is a moral and spiritual one. Protecting children from harm is at the core of biblical justice, and christians have a duty to speak out against any system that seeks to exploit or confuse them.

Educate the Congregation, pastors and church leaders must be willing to inform their congregations about what is happening in schools. Many christians are simply unaware of the depth of the problem and need guidance on how to respond. Churches can hold seminars, distribute resources, and encourage open dialogue on these issues.

Churches should come alongside parents, offering support, prayer, and practical resources to help them navigate these challenging times. This should include helping parents understand their rights in the school system. Church members should be on every school board, also providing alternative educational options like homeschooling or christian schools.

Churches should become involved in local and state politics by encouraging members to run for school boards, vote for family friendly policies, and speak out against harmful curriculums. Christians are called to be salt and light in the world, and this includes the education system.

It is crucial for churches to develop programs that promote biblical values of identity and sexuality for their own children. Sunday school, youth groups, and church sponsored events can serve as places where children learn the truth about who they are in God's eyes and how to navigate the cultural messages they encounter.

The sexualization of children in public schools is one of the most urgent issues of our time, and the church cannot afford to remain silent. As a voice for truth and righteousness, the church must rise up to protect the most vulnerable and push back against the cultural forces that seek to harm them. There is no excuse for inaction, and the longer the church waits, the more ground is lost. Now is the time for boldness, courage, and a commitment to defending children from the moral and spiritual decay that threatens to steal their innocence.

CHAPTER 5 :

Invasion Of The Free World. The Cost Of Silence

Before we move any further, let's be crystal clear about one thing, when God judges a nation, it's never because of the pagans, the unbelievers, or the folks who don't know Him. It's always because of His people. Let that sink in. Throughout the Bible, over and over again, God judges His people, because they knew the truth, and yet, they stayed silent, compromised, or outright rebelled.

Look at Israel. Time and again, God didn't pour out judgment because of the foreign nations. No, it was because of Israel's unfaithfulness. The temple was destroyed, not because the Babylonians were pagans, but because God's people were bowing to idols, ignoring His commands, and turning a blind eye to the corruption in their own midst. Judgment always begins with the house of God. It's not the outside world that brings down a nation, it's the silent, complicit, compromising people of God who fail to stand up against evil.

And here we are today, living in a nation that is spiraling into moral chaos. Is it the fault of the atheists, the Marxists, the radicals? You'd like to think so, wouldn't you? But no, the real problem is that christians have abandoned their post. The church has grown silent, satisfied with its comfort and security while evil flourishes unchecked. And while we sit quietly in our pews, praying for revival, we forget that God's judgment isn't waiting on the world to get worse, it's waiting on His people to wake up.

You see we love to talk about the power of God. We sing about it, preach about it, but do we really understand it? If christians would stop retreating into the shadows, if we would actually rise up and be faithful to God's Word, we could unleash a power this world has never seen. And I'm not talking about some feel good, emotional experience. I'm talking about the raw, world shaking, mountain moving power of God that's more potent than anything you could ever imagine. Stronger than a nuclear bomb? Absolutely.

Let's be real, Elon Musk is a brilliant man. The innovations coming out of Tesla, SpaceX, and Neuralink are staggering. But guess what? God's power puts all of that to shame. As amazing as Musk's achievements are, they're nothing compared to what the people of God could do if they tapped into the power of the Holy Spirit and stood boldly for truth.

Imagine if every christian, across this nation, spoke out against evil with conviction. Imagine if we stopped making excuses, stopped hiding behind weak theology, and stopped pretending that our silence was somehow righteous. If we truly believed what we say we believe, that God's Word is living and active, sharper than any double edged sword, then we'd wield it like the weapon it is. And let me tell you, that kind of power? It's a force greater than all the technology, innovation, and brilliance this world can offer.

The truth is, God's power isn't limited by anything, least of all, the excuses christians use to avoid confronting evil. His power doesn't just change nations, it brings them to their knees. But we've forgotten that. We look at the rise of men like Musk and marvel at what human ingenuity can accomplish. Meanwhile, we forget that the God of the universe, the one who created Musk's very mind, is offering His people a power that is far beyond what any human could ever dream up.

But here's the kicker, it's not that we can't access this power, it's that we don't. We're too busy trying to be "culturally relevant" or "non confrontational." We're too concerned with how the world sees us, and not concerned enough with how God sees us. And that's where the judgment comes in. God doesn't judge us because the world is evil. He judges us because we've failed to stand against it. Because we've failed to use the power He's given us.

Do we honestly think we can stand before God one day and say, "Well, Lord, at least Elon Musk was out there doing great things for humanity"? No, God isn't going to ask us what we thought about SpaceX. He's going to ask why we didn't speak up, why we didn't fight for righteousness, why we sat silently while our nation crumbled around us.

We've been given something far greater than the greatest minds of this age. The power of God is in our hands. But it's only unleashed when we step out in faith, when we speak truth, when we refuse to back down in the face of evil. If we keep silent, the rocks will cry out. And honestly, it looks like we're just about to that point.

Across the globe, borders are becoming increasingly porous, leading to a surge of illegal immigration into many free nations, including the United States. While immigration is a complex issue with humanitarian dimensions, the unregulated flow of people presents significant challenges to national security, economic stability, and cultural cohesion. Yet, in the face of these concerns, much of the church remains silent or unwilling to address the issue head on. This chapter examines how the church's reluctance to speak up about illegal immigration is contributing to an "invasion" of the free world, and how this silence could have long term consequences.

In the book America's Covert Border War by Todd Bensman, a gripping story unfolds about a small Texas town that found itself at the center of the border crisis, and how the lives of ordinary citizens were drastically altered by the sudden influx of migrants. The story centers on Brooks County, a rural community located about 70 miles north of the U.S. Mexico border, which had long been a quiet farming area known for its cattle ranches and wide open spaces. But with the surge in illegal immigration, the town quickly became a focal point for human smuggling, and the local residents found themselves grappling with the consequences of a border crisis they had little control over.

Brooks County is home to the infamous Falfurrias border patrol checkpoint, one of the last barriers between the Texas borderlands and the interior of the United States. This checkpoint is a key point of entry for smugglers attempting to transport migrants deeper into the U.S. To avoid detection at the checkpoint, smugglers often force migrants to trek through the rugged and unforgiving terrain of the surrounding ranch lands, leaving many to die in the desert from dehydration, heat exhaustion, and exposure. This practice transformed Brooks County into what Bensman describes as a "graveyard for migrants."

The story focuses on the experiences of local ranchers, like a man named Mike Vickers, whose once peaceful life was turned upside down by the crisis. Vickers, a veterinarian by trade, owned a ranch that sprawled over thousands of acres of scrubland just outside the town. For generations, his family had lived on and worked the land, never worrying about anything beyond the usual concerns of farm life. But starting in the mid 2000s, Vickers began to notice an alarming increase in the number of migrants crossing his property. What began as a few isolated incidents quickly escalated into a flood of desperate people moving through his land, often under the cover of night.

The scale of the problem became clear when Vickers began finding the bodies. At first, it was a few here and there, people who had succumbed to the harsh conditions while trying to evade border patrol. But as the years went by, the number of bodies grew. Migrants who had been abandoned by their smugglers, known as "coyotes," or who had simply become lost in the desert, were dying in record numbers. Vickers and other ranchers would often come across decomposing remains or skeletons while out working their land. These grim discoveries took a toll on the local community, as the small county lacked the resources to deal with the bodies or to address the broader humanitarian crisis unfolding in their backyard.

In one particularly harrowing incident described in the book, Vickers found the body of a young woman who had been left behind by her group. She had clearly been struggling to survive for days, with nothing more than an empty water bottle and a tattered backpack by her side. The sight of her lifeless body haunted Vickers, and he couldn't help but wonder what she must have gone through in her final hours. It was a stark reminder of the human cost of the border crisis, a tragedy that was playing out in his own backyard.

But it wasn't just the bodies that troubled Vickers and his neighbors. The sheer volume of migrants moving through their land created constant disruptions to their lives. Property damage became a regular occurrence, as migrants would break into homes and barns looking for food, water, or shelter. Fences were cut, cattle were stolen, and equipment was vandalized. Some ranchers even began carrying firearms at all times, fearful for their safety after hearing stories of violent encounters with smugglers. The once peaceful community was now living in a state of high alert, with residents feeling abandoned by their own government, which seemed unable or unwilling to stem the tide of illegal immigration.

In response, Vickers and other ranchers formed a group called the Texas Border Volunteers. The group's goal was to patrol their land and provide assistance to Border Patrol agents who were often overwhelmed by the sheer volume of migrants crossing the border. Armed with rifles and night vision goggles, they would spend hours each night scanning their land for signs of illegal crossings. They weren't vigilantes they insisted, they weren't there to apprehend or harm anyone, just to monitor and report suspicious activity to border patrol. But the fact that they felt the need to take matters into their own hands spoke volumes about the government's failure to secure the border.

As the crisis intensified, Brooks County became a national symbol of the humanitarian and security issues caused by unchecked illegal immigration. Local law enforcement, already stretched thin, struggled to keep up with the demands placed on them by the constant flow of migrants. The county's small medical examiner's office was overwhelmed by the number of bodies being recovered, often lacking the resources to properly identify or even bury the dead. The community, once a quiet rural enclave, found itself on the front lines of a crisis that had implications far beyond its borders.

For Vickers and the other residents of Brooks County, the border crisis was not just a political issue, it was an everyday reality that they could not escape. They saw firsthand the human suffering caused by illegal immigration, and they also bore the brunt of the government's failure to enforce its own laws. The story of Brooks County, as told by Todd Bensman, serves as a stark reminder that the border crisis is not just about numbers or statistics, it is about real people, on both sides of the border, who are being affected in profound and often tragic ways.

This story from America's Covert Border War highlights the broader themes of this book, particularly the need for moral courage in confronting societal issues. Just as the church in Nazi Germany failed to speak out against the atrocities happening in their own backyard, the church today risks becoming complicit in the current border crisis by remaining silent or indifferent. The people of Brooks County, like the church, found themselves at a moral crossroads, would they stand by and allow the crisis to continue, or would they take action to defend their community and uphold the rule of law?

The story also serves as a reminder that the consequences of inaction are not theoretical. The human cost of the border crisis is real, and it is being felt by ordinary people like Mike Vickers, whose lives have been forever changed by the events playing out on the U.S. Mexico border. As the crisis continues, the church must decide whether it will stand up and confront the issue head on, or whether it will remain silent, allowing the suffering to continue.

Illegal immigration is not just a political issue, it has far reaching societal implications. When borders are not respected or properly regulated, it undermines the rule of law, creates vulnerabilities in national security, and places enormous pressure on public services like healthcare, education, and housing. In the United States, for example, there has been a sharp increase in illegal immigration, leading to overwhelmed border patrols, strained resources, and a rise in human trafficking and drug smuggling.

Moreover, unregulated immigration threatens to erode the cultural and moral fabric of a nation. A country's values, customs, and laws shape its identity, and when these are disregarded, the social cohesion necessary for a functioning society begins to break down. Despite these pressing concerns, many churches remain either indifferent or overly cautious about addressing the immigration crisis.

A large part of the church's hesitation stems from a well intentioned but misguided understanding of compassion. Many christian leaders, in an effort to show love and grace, argue that we should welcome all immigrants, regardless of legal status, because they are made in the image of God. While it is true that every human being bears God's image and deserves dignity, this does not mean that governments should ignore illegal immigration or fail to enforce just laws.

Romans 13:1-7 clearly states that God has ordained governments to maintain order and enforce the law. Allowing unregulated immigration undermines the authority of the state and disrespects those who seek to immigrate legally. True compassion must be balanced with justice, and it is not compassionate to turn a blind eye to the exploitation of immigration systems which often leads to human suffering. Such as human trafficking, exploitation of workers, and the breaking down of families.

Furthermore, the church's silence on illegal immigration often fails to consider the well being of the citizens of the host country. Unregulated immigration can lead to economic strain, job competition, and social unrest, particularly in poorer communities. As christians, we are called to love our neighbors both the immigrant and the citizen and that means advocating for policies that protect the dignity of all involved.

One of the most significant concerns about illegal immigration is its impact on national security. In the absence of proper border enforcement, countries become vulnerable to terrorist infiltration, drug cartels, and other criminal elements. The southern border of the United States, for example, has seen an influx of drugs, particularly fentanyl, which is responsible for thousands of overdose deaths annually. Additionally, human trafficking rings exploit the chaos at the border, victimizing countless women and children.

By refusing to address these issues, the church is failing in its prophetic role to protect the vulnerable and promote justice. National security is not simply a political issue, it is a matter of protecting innocent lives from harm. The bible speaks repeatedly about the role of the righteous in promoting peace and justice within society, Proverbs 29:4. When the church refuses to speak out on issues that threaten the safety of the nation, it neglects its responsibility to be a voice for justice.

One of the more subtle but equally significant consequences of unregulated immigration is the erosion of a nation's cultural and moral foundations. Every society is built upon shared values, laws, and traditions. When a country experiences unchecked immigration without integration, the cohesiveness of these values begins to break down. In the case of the United States, which was founded on principles of liberty, justice, and individual rights, the influx of people who do not share these values can lead to cultural fragmentation. Take for example Dearborn Michigan. In recent years, Dearborn, Michigan, has been the epicenter of several rallies where participants have expressed anti American sentiments. A notable instance occurred in April 2024 during the annual Al Quds Day rally, an event established by the late Ayatollah Khomeini to oppose Israeli governance over Jerusalem.

During this rally, a significant number of participants chanted slogans such as "Death to America" and "Death to Israel." Speakers at the event voiced strong anti Israel and anti American rhetoric. Imam Usama Abdulghani referred to Israel as a "cancer" and equated it with ISIS and Nazi Germany. He asserted that Israel is an "evil settler colonialist project" and proclaimed that "the people of the world now know this."

Another speaker, activist Tarek Bazzi, criticized the U.S. political system, stating that not only does "Genocide Joe" have to go, but "the entire US system has to go." He echoed Malcolm X's sentiment by declaring, "We live in one of the rottenest countries that has ever existed on this earth."

These events have sparked concern and condemnation within the broader community. Dr. Mahmoud Al Hadidi, chairman of the Michigan Muslim Community Council, emphasized that such chants do not represent the views of Muslims in the United States and advocated for an investigation into the matter.

The prevalence of such rallies and the sentiments expressed have also influenced the political dynamics in Michigan. The Muslim and Arab American communities, which have been pivotal in electoral outcomes, have shown signs of shifting their political allegiances. This shift is attributed to dissatisfaction with U.S. policies, particularly regarding conflicts involving Israel and Gaza.

In response to these concerns, the Biden administration has engaged in efforts to address the grievances of Arab American and Muslim leaders in Michigan. Senior aides have been dispatched to meet with community leaders to discuss U.S. policies and their implications .

These events underscore the importance of understanding and addressing the diverse perspectives within the Muslim community in Michigan, especially regarding U.S. domestic and foreign policies

Biblical values, such as the sanctity of life, the importance of family, and personal responsibility, are essential to the health of any nation. When these values are undermined, society begins to unravel. The church should be concerned about the preservation of these values, as they are rooted in biblical truth. By remaining silent on the cultural impact of unregulated immigration, the church allows for the erosion of the very principles that protect freedom and justice in society.

The church's silence on immigration is not only a failure to engage with a pressing social issue, it is also a missed opportunity to provide biblical wisdom and leadership. The Bible offers a balanced perspective on immigration, one that emphasizes both compassion for the foreigner and respect for the law. In Leviticus 19:33-34, the Israelites were commanded to treat foreigners with kindness and fairness, but this was within the context of a lawful society with clear rules and regulations.

The church must reclaim its prophetic voice in this area, offering a message that upholds the dignity of immigrants while also respecting the rule of law. This requires a willingness to engage with political and social realities, even when doing so is unpopular. The church is not called to avoid difficult conversations, it is called to speak truth in love, Ephesians 4:15.

While some may see this as a political issue, border security is a matter of justice and protection. The church can support policies that protect vulnerable populations from exploitation by criminal elements, while also advocating for humane treatment of those caught in illegal immigration.

 Christians should not shy away from political involvement on this issue. Voting for policies that promote the rule of law and protect national security is part of our responsibility as citizens and believers.

The invasion of the free world through illegal immigration is not just a political crisis, it is a moral and spiritual one. The church's silence on this issue has allowed it to grow unchecked, with dire consequences for both the immigrants involved and the citizens of the nations affected. Now is the time for the church to speak up, offering a voice of compassion balanced with wisdom and justice.

Christians are called to love their neighbors, uphold the law, and protect the vulnerable. This means addressing immigration in a way that respects both the dignity of immigrants and the sovereignty of nations. The free world, built on principles of freedom and justice, is at risk of losing its foundations, and the church cannot afford to remain silent. It must rise to the occasion, offering leadership and moral clarity in these troubled times.

CHAPTER 6 :

The Johnson Amendment: A Bad Deal For The Church

The Johnson Amendment, passed in 1954, has been a point of contention for many within the christian community, especially those who believe the church should have a strong voice in the political and moral debates of the nation. This legislation, which prohibits tax exempt organizations including churches from endorsing or opposing political candidates, has often been seen as a tool used to silence the church and keep it from speaking on issues that matter most.

I said in my video, The Silence Of The Church.

It was wrong on multiple fronts to agree with that arrangement in the first place but that was a great deal for Satan and his allies. Give the church tax exempt status for keeping their mouth shut. Old Satan is often smarter than we are.

By taking the voice of the church out of the picture it makes his work even easier. By squelching the voice of the church they will break the covenant the founders of this country made with God. It's a win win for the dark side, but it's worse than that.

So while the church took the 30 pieces of silver, to coin a phrase, for the church to keep its bargain with the devil, I mean the state, all the church had to do was not endorse particular candidates. The church could have still been very active and presenting the policies of the candidates, and a much needed positive influence on the direction of our country. But the church gave the state even more for their money, the church for the most part went silent on political matters and focused solely on the gospel, as if separating the two is possible.

This is what Oliver North says in his book Tragic Consequences, "sitting back and letting the anti god crowd take over the political process is not good stewardship. The motto for the christian when it comes to politics should be, engage in the political process but don't depend on it. Politicians will not reclaim the culture for Christ, on the other hand they certainly helped the anti God crowd push Christ out of the culture."

 Indeed they did. So for the most part, the most political we get in today's church, is to talk to people before and after service around election time about who we plan to vote for, and we can expect little to nothing said from the pulpit. Any discussion we do get from the pulpit about culture and political matters is usually very vague.

So while our tax dollars go for sexualizing our kids in public schools and providing abortions for girls as young as 12 years old without informing their parents. Doctor assisted suicide, millions of unvetted people and dangerous drugs pouring into our southern border, and our religious rights taken away the church remains mostly silent and goes about business as usual. I don't know about you, but I see a problem with that.

In this chapter, we'll explore the history and impact of the Johnson Amendment, why many believe it was a bad deal for the church, and how it has contributed to the weakening of the church's influence in society. Most importantly, we will discuss why the church should never have allowed itself to be silenced and how it can reclaim its prophetic voice, even within the constraints of modern laws.

The Johnson Amendment was introduced by then Senator Lyndon B. Johnson as part of a broader tax reform bill in 1954. Its purpose was to prevent non profit organizations, including churches, from engaging in political campaigning or endorsing candidates while maintaining their tax exempt status. Though it was framed as a way to protect the integrity of charitable organizations and prevent them from becoming too political. The amendment had a chilling effect on churches, discouraging them from speaking out on political issues for fear of losing their tax exempt status.

The church, at the time, did little to push back against this legislation. Many pastors and church leaders believed that staying out of politics was not only wise but also in line with their mission to focus on spiritual matters. However, this separation of faith and politics has had significant consequences for the church and the broader culture.

Since the passage of the Johnson Amendment, many churches have been hesitant to speak out on political issues, especially during election cycles. The fear of losing tax exempt status has led to a kind of self censorship, where pastors avoid discussing moral and political issues from the pulpit, even when those issues directly affect their congregations, and the nation as a whole. This has allowed many harmful ideologies to spread unchecked, as the church has removed itself from the public square.

The church's reluctance to address political issues has had a profound effect on society. Issues such as abortion, same sex marriage, religious freedom, and the sanctity of life have become battlegrounds where the church's voice is notably absent. Without strong moral leadership, these debates are dominated by secular voices that often promote values directly opposed to biblical teachings.

Moreover, by staying silent on these critical issues, the church has allowed its moral authority to be diminished. In a culture where moral relativism reigns, the absence of a clear, biblical voice on key issues has led many to view the church as irrelevant to modern life. This has contributed to the overall decline in church influence and attendance, particularly among younger generations who are looking for guidance on how to navigate the moral complexities of the modern world.

Throughout Scripture, God's people have been called to speak truth to power. Prophets like Isaiah, Jeremiah, and Amos were not afraid to confront kings and rulers when they strayed from God's commandments. John the Baptist was executed for daring to confront Herod about his immoral actions. Even Jesus Himself was not afraid to challenge the political and religious authorities of His day when they failed to uphold God's truth.

The idea that the church should remain silent on political matters is foreign to the Bible. While the church's primary mission is spiritual, it also has a responsibility to promote justice, defend the oppressed, and uphold the moral order that God has established. When the church refuses to engage in these areas, it fails to fulfill its role as the salt and light of the world, Matthew 5:13-16.

Romans 13 teaches that government is instituted by God to promote good and restrain evil. However, when government strays from its divine purpose, whether by promoting immorality, oppressing the weak, or silencing the church, it is the church's responsibility to call it to account. The Johnson Amendment has created an environment where the church feels constrained in its ability to fulfill this role, and that is a problem that must be addressed.

One of the greatest mistakes the church made was accepting the limitations imposed by the Johnson Amendment without a fight. While the law specifically prohibits endorsing or opposing candidates, it has been interpreted more broadly by many churches as a restriction on all political speech. This has led to an environment where the church is often afraid to even discuss moral issues that have political implications.

The church should never have allowed itself to be muzzled in this way. There are several reasons why the church should reject the constraints of the Johnson Amendment.

At its core, the gospel is about the establishment of God's kingdom, which has direct implications for how societies are governed. Issues like justice, human dignity, and morality are not just spiritual concerns, they are political ones as well. The church cannot faithfully proclaim the full gospel if it refuses to engage with the political realities of the world.

Many of the most pressing moral issues of our time, abortion, euthanasia, religious liberty, and marriage, are also political issues. The church cannot be silent on these matters without abandoning its responsibility to speak truth into the culture.

Historically, the church has been a leading voice in movements for social justice and moral reform, from the abolition of slavery to the civil rights movement. By allowing the Johnson Amendment to silence it, the church has abdicated its role as a moral compass for the nation.

The good news is that the church can reclaim its prophetic voice, even within the constraints of the Johnson Amendment. While the amendment restricts churches from endorsing specific candidates, it does not prevent them from speaking on moral issues that are central to the political debates of our time.

Pastors must not shy away from preaching on difficult topics simply because they have political implications. Issues like abortion, marriage, justice, and religious freedom are biblical issues, and the church must teach what the Bible says about them.

Churches can provide resources and educational opportunities for their congregants to learn more about how their faith applies to political and social issues. This can include voter guides, forums, and discussions on current events through a biblical lens.

While the church must operate within the law, it can also advocate for the repeal or reform of laws that restrict its ability to speak freely. There is a growing movement to repeal the Johnson Amendment, and churches can support this effort through prayer, education, and advocacy.

Churches can encourage their members to be politically active, whether by voting, running for office, or engaging in grassroots advocacy. Christians are called to be good stewards of their influence, and that includes participating in the political process. Donald Trump addressed the issue of the Johnson Amendment during a speech at the National Prayer Breakfast on February 2, 2017. He emphasized his commitment to repealing the Johnson Amendment, which prohibits tax exempt organizations, including churches, from endorsing political candidates or engaging in political campaigning.

Additionally, Donald Trump spoke about this topic at the Faith and Freedom Coalition's Road to Majority Conference on June 8, 2017, where he reiterated his support for the repeal, appealing to evangelical leaders and emphasizing the importance of religious freedom. Throughout his presidency, Trump frequently mentioned the Johnson Amendment in the context of empowering churches and religious organizations to engage more freely in political discourse.

The reactions from church leaders to Donald Trump's calls for the repeal of the Johnson Amendment were mixed.

 Some evangelical leaders welcomed the idea, viewing the repeal as a way to enhance religious freedom. They argued that the amendment stifled the ability of churches to speak out on social and political issues that align with their beliefs. Leaders like Jerry Falwell Jr., president of Liberty University, openly supported Trump's stance, advocating for a more active role of churches in political matters.

Other church leaders expressed caution. They feared that repealing the Johnson Amendment might lead to the politicization of churches, potentially alienating congregants who hold differing political views. Leaders like Russell Moore, president of the Ethics & Religious Liberty Commission of the Southern Baptist Convention, argued that while they wanted the freedom to speak out, they were concerned that endorsing candidates could compromise the church's mission and integrity.

Many mainline protestant leaders and denominations opposed the repeal. They argued that the Johnson Amendment protects the church's prophetic voice and its ability to speak truth to power without being co opted by partisan politics. This group often emphasized the importance of maintaining a clear separation between church and state.

Overall, while some evangelical leaders supported Trump's initiative, others raised concerns about the implications for the church's role in society and its relationship with political power.

The reality is, that God is inherently political. It was God not humanity, who established the framework of governance, setting rulers and authorities in place (Romans 13:1). Heaven and hell aren't symbolic, they are the literal destinations of all mankind, not depending whether we believe in them or not. Divine declarations of good and evil aren't subject to a majority opinion. God doesn't check polls before defining right and wrong, nor does He pause to see if anyone's offended. His standards are absolute, whether people like it or not.

It's past time for the church to stop dancing around hard truths, afraid of losing cultural approval. The message isn't complicated. God has drawn the lines, and silence isn't a virtue when those lines are under attack. If the church won't unite around the unchanging truths of heaven, hell, and divine authority, who will? We aren't called to whisper truth from the sidelines. The world is spiraling, and the time to speak up is now.

CHAPTER 7 :

God Is In Control: The Church's Go To Excuse For Inaction

One of the most frequently heard phrases in christian circles, particularly when confronting societal or political issues is, "God is in control." While this statement is theologically true, it is often used as a justification for inaction. Many believers use this truth as a way to detach from the world's problems, convinced that their involvement isn't necessary because God will work things out without their participation. This chapter will examine how this mindset undermines the church's responsibility and diminishes its impact on the culture.

The Bible is clear that God is sovereign over all creation. He is the King of kings, the Lord of lords, and He directs the course of history according to His divine plan, Proverbs 19:21, Isaiah 46:9-10. However, God's sovereignty does not negate human responsibility. In fact, the Bible repeatedly emphasizes the importance of human action in fulfilling God's purposes on earth.

From the time of Adam and Eve in the Garden of Eden, God has invited humans to partner with Him in stewarding His creation and advancing His kingdom. Throughout Scripture, we see that God often works through His people to accomplish His will. Whether it's Moses leading the Israelites out of Egypt, Esther standing up to save her people, or the apostles spreading the gospel, human action is a critical part of God's unfolding plan.

Unfortunately, some christians use the doctrine of God's sovereignty as an excuse for passivity, forgetting that while God is in control, He also calls us to act. This mindset can lead to a hands off approach that leaves the world's problems to worsen, all while christians wait for God to intervene.

Albert Einstein said, "the world will not be destroyed by those who do evil, but by those who watch them without doing anything."

While the phrase "God is in control" is often used to comfort and reassure, it should never be used to absolve us from our responsibility to engage with the world. The Bible calls believers to be salt and light, Matthew 5:13-16, to do justice, love mercy, and walk humbly with God, Micah 6:8, and to fight against evil and stand for truth, Ephesians 6:10-18.

When the church disengages, believing that God will fix everything without its involvement, it misses the biblical mandate to be an active force for good in society. The idea that God will handle everything without requiring our participation is a distortion of His sovereign plan. Yes, God is in control, but He also calls His people to take responsibility for the world they live in and to act as His hands and feet on the earth.

Consider the story of Nehemiah, who, upon hearing of the desolation of Jerusalem, did not sit back and say, "God is in control." Instead, he wept, fasted, prayed, and then took decisive action. Nehemiah trusted God's sovereignty, but he also understood that God wanted him to be an active participant in the restoration of Jerusalem, Nehemiah 1-2.

Similarly, throughout history, christians have led movements for justice, reform, and revival. From the abolition of slavery to the civil rights movement, believers who understood that God is in control also understood that they had a role to play in bringing about His purposes on earth. Their actions were guided by faith, but their faith did not lead to inaction.

The passive belief that "God is in control" can lead to dangerous complacency. In times of moral, political, or social crisis, christians must be the first to stand up for truth, justice, and righteousness. When we fail to act, evil flourishes. The church's silence or inactivity in the face of injustice allows destructive ideologies and practices to take root in society.

For example, the hyper grace movement, which downplays the importance of obedience and repentance, often promotes the idea that God's grace covers all, regardless of human response or responsibility. This theology can lead believers to adopt a passive, laissez faire attitude toward sin and societal decay, believing that God will take care of it all in the end. However, such a view ignores the biblical call to action, repentance, and engagement in the world.

We see this same passivity in the church's response to political and cultural challenges today. Many christians, rather than engaging in the public square, choose to retreat, comforted by the belief that God is in control and will work everything out in His time. But history shows that when the church retreats, evil advances.

It's essential to strike a balance between trusting in God's sovereignty and fulfilling our responsibility to act. James 2:26 reminds us that faith without works is dead. True faith compels action. If we genuinely believe that God is sovereign, we should be emboldened to act, knowing that He is ultimately in control of the outcomes. Our responsibility is to be faithful stewards of the opportunities and influence He has given us.

One of the clearest examples of this balance is found in the Great Commission, Matthew 28:18-20. Jesus, who has been given all authority in heaven and on earth, commands His followers to go and make disciples of all nations. He promises to be with us always, yet He still calls us to go, teach, and baptize. God's sovereignty does not eliminate our responsibility, it empowers and compels us to act with confidence, knowing that He is guiding and sustaining us in our mission.

The church must not fall into the trap of thinking that because God is in control, its involvement in the world is unnecessary. Instead, the knowledge of God's sovereignty should inspire christians to engage more fully in the work of advancing His kingdom. Whether it's speaking out against injustice, standing up for biblical values, or participating in the political process, believers are called to be active participants in God's plan.

To avoid falling into the trap of passivity, the church must adopt a mindset of action. Here are a few practical steps that can help believers engage more effectively in the world.

Prayer is essential, but it must be coupled with action. Believers should be praying for wisdom, guidance, and strength to engage with the world's problems, but they should also be looking for practical ways to make a difference in their communities.

Churches need to educate their congregations about the pressing moral, political, and social issues of the day and equip them to respond in a biblical manner. This can include hosting forums, offering voter guides, and encouraging civic engagement.

Christians are called to be salt and light in the world, preserving what is good and shining the light of truth in the darkness. This means engaging in culture, politics, education, and other areas where biblical values are under attack.

The church must be willing to speak out against injustice and stand up for those who cannot stand up for themselves. Whether it's advocating for the unborn, defending religious freedom, or opposing immoral laws, the church has a responsibility to be a voice for truth.

Finally, believers must trust in God's sovereignty but also understand that they are called to act. God often works through His people to accomplish His purposes, and He has given the church a mandate to engage with the world and make a difference.

In Seth Gruber's book, The 1916 Project, he critically examines the passive mindset prevalent among many christians, particularly the tendency to use the phrase "God is in control" as a justification for inaction amidst moral and societal decline. Gruber argues that while acknowledging God's sovereignty, christians are called to be proactive agents of change, confronting injustices such as abortion and the erosion of religious freedoms.

He contends that this passive attitude has led to significant inaction within the church, especially regarding issues like abortion and the erosion of religious freedoms. Gruber points out that many believers use the phrase "God is in control" to absolve themselves of responsibility, suggesting that if they truly embraced God's sovereignty, they would recognize their role in actively opposing evil and promoting righteousness.

By remaining passive, the church inadvertently allows the proliferation of injustice and the suffering of innocents. Gruber emphasizes that true faith in God's control should compel believers to engage actively in societal issues, reflecting God's love and justice in tangible ways.

While it's comforting to know that "God is in control," this truth should never be used as an excuse for inaction. The Bible is clear that while God is sovereign, He also calls His people to act. The church must not retreat from the world's problems, but rather engage with them, trusting that God will work through its efforts to bring about His purposes.

By reclaiming a theology of action, the church can once again become a powerful force for good in society. God is indeed in control, but He has also entrusted His people with the responsibility to work for justice, truth, and righteousness in the world. It's time for the church to step up and fulfill that calling.

CHAPTER 8 :

Faces Behind the Fall: The Architects of Our Decline

There are many forms of evil, and sometimes evil works subtly, hiding in omission or silence. It's not always loud and obvious. I have no doubt that the real faces behind the fall must begin with the pastors and church leaders who, over the years, went silent on critical political and social issues, choosing instead to focus solely on what they claim is "the Gospel." The Gospel is far more all encompassing, it's not just about personal salvation but about speaking against evil and standing for truth, wherever it shows up. Silence in the face of evil is complicity, and the church's refusal to engage has left a moral vacuum filled by destructive forces.

If we were to look back to the Garden of Eden and assign faces to that first fall, Satan would certainly be the obvious culprit. But Adam and Eve weren't guiltless, they stood by, participated, and ultimately faced judgment alongside the serpent. In the same way, the church's leaders have had a role in this current fall by standing idly by while society unraveled. So, it's only fitting to begin this chapter by naming those who stayed silent when they should have spoken out, those entrusted to shepherd the flock but chose comfort over courage, leaving the door open for evil to run rampant.

Randi Weingarten, the long time president of the American Federation of Teachers, has played a controversial role in the shaping of modern American education. Her tenure, marked by fierce political activism and an uncompromising stance on certain key issues, has made her one of the most polarizing figures in the public education system. One of the most glaring examples of her influence is how the teachers' unions, under her leadership, became instrumental in shaping policies that have fundamentally altered the trajectory of education in the United States.

Weingarten is married to Rabbi Sharon Kleinbaum, a lesbian rabbi who leads Congregation Beit Simchat Torah in New York, a synagogue known for its outreach to the LGBTQ community. Their partnership reflects Weingarten's commitment to LGBTQ advocacy, both in her personal life and through her professional platforms. This dynamic has further positioned her as a prominent figure in progressive activism, supporting social causes that intersect with education and labor rights.

The role of Weingarten during the COVID-19 pandemic stands as a key chapter in her legacy. As schools across the nation grappled with how to proceed with education amidst the uncertainties of the pandemic, Randi Weingarten and the AFT pushed for policies that would have significant long term consequences. In the midst of intense debate over whether to reopen schools or keep them closed, Weingarten strongly advocated for extended closures, citing safety concerns for both students and teachers. While the health risks were indeed a concern, critics argued that Weingarten's stance was not purely motivated by safety but was heavily influenced by political considerations.

Throughout the pandemic, Weingarten and the AFT were seen as closely aligned with Democratic politicians and progressive ideologies, which many argue resulted in prolonged school closures that disproportionately impacted low income and minority students. Parents and education advocates began to voice frustrations, accusing the AFT of putting politics above the educational needs of children. They pointed out that many private and charter schools, as well as schools in other countries, reopened much earlier and did not experience the dire outcomes predicted by Weingarten and the unions.

Beyond the pandemic, Weingarten has also been a key figure in supporting curriculum changes that have sparked national debates. The AFT, under her leadership, has been a strong proponent of incorporating progressive ideas into school curricula, including teachings on critical race theory and comprehensive sex education. While many view these as necessary steps toward a more inclusive and equitable education system, others argue that they have contributed to the growing divide in the country and the politicization of public education.

One particular issue that has drawn immense backlash is Weingarten's stance on parental rights and involvement in education. In various statements and public appearances, she has pushed back against the notion that parents should have a decisive say in what is taught in schools. Her famous assertion that "parents aren't the curriculum experts" inflamed an already tense situation. Parents across the nation began to feel alienated and powerless in the face of what they saw as a system run by union leaders like Weingarten who, they believed, did not have the best interests of their children at heart.

Weingarten's influence goes beyond just education policies, she has wielded considerable power in political circles. Under her leadership, the AFT became a major financial backer of left leaning politicians, ensuring that her vision for education was closely tied to the progressive political agenda. This has led to accusations that Weingarten and the AFT have prioritized politics over education, using their influence to steer the country in a direction that many believe is detrimental to both the education system and the nation's future.

Despite the criticisms, Weingarten remains a formidable figure in American education. Her supporters argue that she is fighting for the safety and rights of teachers, and that the policies she promotes are necessary for addressing systemic inequalities in the education system. Yet, for her detractors, Weingarten embodies much of what they see as wrong with the modern education system, politicized, detached from parental concerns, and focused on ideological indoctrination rather than academic excellence.

In the book Hide Your Children by Liz Wheeler, Randi Weingarten, the president of the American Federation of Teachers, is portrayed as a significant player in the agenda that has infiltrated America's public school system. Wheeler dives into the power dynamics that Weingarten wields over education and the influence she has in shaping the minds of the nation's children, often without parental consent or awareness.

Weingarten's role is more than just that of a union leader advocating for better pay and conditions for teachers. According to Wheeler, she has been instrumental in pushing a progressive agenda that is transforming schools into hubs of social and political indoctrination. One of the most controversial aspects of this shift is the introduction of critical race theory into classrooms, a curriculum that divides students along racial lines and promotes the idea that America's institutions are inherently racist. Weingarten has been a vocal defender of CRT, even going so far as to threaten lawsuits against those who try to ban its teaching, all while dismissing parental concerns as politically motivated.

Wheeler also sheds light on how Weingarten and the AFT have pushed comprehensive sex education that introduces children to sexual concepts and gender ideology at younger and younger ages. The influence of Weingarten's union has been instrumental in developing curricula that many parents find deeply concerning, as they often promote gender fluidity, transgenderism, and sexual freedom under the guise of inclusivity and equality. This has caused an uproar among parents who feel their rights to guide their children's moral education are being stripped away by bureaucratic leaders like Weingarten.

A key moment discussed in Wheeler's book was Weingarten's involvement during the COVID-19 pandemic, where she used her power to keep schools closed for extended periods. Wheeler points out that this was not done solely for health reasons, but as a way to increase the union's political clout. The prolonged closures had disastrous effects on children's education, especially among low income and minority families, yet Weingarten was more focused on maintaining political power than addressing these inequities. The widespread learning loss and mental health crises that arose from extended remote schooling were ignored by the union under her leadership. Instead of prioritizing the well being of students, the AFT, under Weingarten's direction, pushed back against reopening plans while promoting their broader agenda.

In Hide Your Children, Wheeler argues that Weingarten represents a dangerous trend in which unions like the AFT have essentially hijacked the education system. These unions have become conduits for political activism, leaving parents and communities feeling disempowered and disconnected from what happens in their local schools. Weingarten's actions, according to Wheeler, have contributed to a growing divide between parents and educators, as unions increasingly view parents as obstacles to be overcome rather than partners in education.

Randi Weingarten's influence as the president of the American Federation of Teachers has had a profound and controversial impact on the American education system. Her leadership has not only shaped policies around labor rights but has also deeply affected what children are being taught in classrooms across the nation, contributing to the politicization of education. Over the years, Weingarten has expanded the union's focus beyond traditional labor issues, advocating for progressive social policies that have caused significant backlash among parents, educators, and policymakers alike.

Weingarten's influence didn't stop at reopening policies. Under her leadership, the AFT became a powerful force in promoting progressive curricula in public schools, including the adoption of critical race theory and gender ideology. She championed initiatives that reframed history through the lens of systemic oppression and promoted discussions on race and privilege, even at the elementary level. Parents who raised concerns about these teachings were often dismissed or labeled as extremists. Weingarten downplayed the backlash, suggesting that parents were being manipulated by right wing media, further alienating families who felt excluded from decisions about their children's education.

In addition to CRT, Weingarten supported the inclusion of comprehensive sex education that introduces topics of sexual identity and gender fluidity at increasingly younger ages. The AFT has backed policies that allow schools to provide counseling and support for children questioning their gender, often without parental knowledge or consent. These policies have caused widespread outrage among parents, many of whom believe that such decisions should remain within the family. Weingarten's stance reflects a broader trend within the union to diminish parental involvement in favor of state controlled education, framing parents as obstacles rather than partners.

Weingarten has also wielded significant political influence, using the AFT's resources to back progressive candidates and causes. The union has donated millions of dollars to campaigns that align with its social agenda, making the AFT a major player in national politics. Critics argue that this shift from education to activism has come at the expense of students, as the focus has moved away from academic achievement toward political and social indoctrination. Weingarten's defense of these policies often comes across as dismissive of parental concerns. Reinforcing the perception that unions are more interested in wielding power than ensuring quality education for children.

Perhaps one of the most telling aspects of Weingarten's leadership is how deeply divided the education landscape has become under her watch.

Charter schools, private schools, and homeschooling have seen significant growth as parents seek alternatives to public education. Many families feeling that public schools no longer align with their values, have taken their children out of the system entirely. Instead of addressing these concerns, Weingarten has doubled down on union priorities, promoting more centralized control over education while dismissing parents who challenge the status quo.

In the end, Weingarten's impact on American education goes far beyond labor issues. Under her leadership, the AFT has transformed from a union focused on protecting teachers to a political machine pushing progressive social policies. The consequences have been profound, declining academic performance, growing distrust between parents and educators, and an exodus from the public school system. Weingarten's legacy is one of power and influence, but it's also one that has left many parents and communities questioning whether public education still serves the best interests of children.

In Hide Your Children by Liz Wheeler, the story of Emily Drabinski's rise to the presidency of the American Library Association reveals how libraries have become battlegrounds for ideological control. Drabinski, a self described Marxist represents a stark shift in the priorities of the ALA, moving beyond traditional roles of promoting literacy and public access to knowledge toward actively pushing progressive and left wing ideologies.

Wheeler emphasizes how Drabinski's leadership aims to reshape libraries into institutions of social activism. Her controversial vision includes using libraries to advance ideas surrounding critical race theory, gender ideology, and socialist organizing. Drabinski's belief that libraries are ideal spaces for such activism has fueled backlash from parents and conservative communities who feel that these efforts undermine parental authority and expose children to inappropriate content.

A key issue Wheeler highlights is Drabinski's endorsement of the inclusion of sexually explicit materials in school and public libraries. She frames any attempt to remove such books as an assault on intellectual freedom. The ALA's official stance under Drabinski's leadership has been to defend these materials, even those that some parents view as harmful or obscene for minors. This policy has led to tense school board meetings, with parents demanding the removal of explicit content and accusing the ALA of promoting ideological indoctrination.

Wheeler argues that Drabinski's tenure epitomizes the cultural battle over education and public spaces. Her Marxist leanings are not just personal beliefs but are reflected in how the ALA promotes certain types of books and events like drag queen story hours, while sidelining or dismissing concerns from parents and communities. The growing controversy around Drabinski has even led some states, like Montana, to sever ties with the ALA altogether, signaling broader resistance to the direction she is taking the organization.

In Hide Your Children, Wheeler connects Drabinski's story to a larger trend of public institutions being co-opted for ideological purposes. She suggests that libraries, once neutral spaces focused on literacy and learning, are now being used as tools for reshaping cultural norms. Drabinski's leadership, according to Wheeler, highlights the importance of parental involvement and vigilance, as the push for progressive ideologies infiltrates even seemingly benign public institutions like libraries.

John Dewey, often called the "father of modern education," was not only a pioneering educational reformer but also a figure whose ideas have had a long lasting and controversial influence on the American education system. Dewey's progressive philosophy rooted in pragmatism, revolutionized how students are taught, moving away from classical education models and toward experiential, student centered learning. However, beyond his educational theories, Dewey was also known for his sympathetic stance toward socialist and Marxist ideas, which raised concerns about the deeper implications of his influence on public education.

Dewey believed that education should do more than transmit knowledge, it should shape citizens for participation in a democratic society. His view was that schools should not only teach facts and figures but also foster critical thinking, collaboration, and social engagement. On the surface, these ideas sound admirable. However, Dewey's vision went further, he saw education as a tool to mold society itself, and in his mind, that society leaned toward collectivism. Dewey was deeply skeptical of individualism, favoring a system in which individuals work toward collective goals, a belief that aligns with socialist thought.

Throughout his career, Dewey's writings and actions reflected sympathy for socialist ideas. He traveled to the Soviet Union in the 1920s, where he observed the education system being shaped under the new communist government. Upon returning, Dewey praised elements of the Soviet system, particularly its emphasis on collective learning and the state's role in shaping the minds of young citizens. While Dewey did not explicitly endorse Soviet communism, his admiration for aspects of their education model was clear. He believed that education should promote not only intellectual growth but also social reform. Something that could challenge the existing political and economic order in America.

Dewey's influence began to permeate American education through the progressive movement, which sought to replace the traditional, teacher centered model with a more student focused approach. His ideas emphasized experiential learning, downplaying memorization and classical knowledge in favor of hands on activities and problem solving skills. While this shift had its benefits, critics argue that Dewey's approach also opened the door for education to become a vehicle for ideological influence, moving away from objective knowledge toward subjective and politically driven content.

Over time, Dewey's educational philosophy evolved into what we now call "progressive education." His theories inspired generations of teachers and administrators, and his emphasis on shaping the "whole child" laid the groundwork for the modern public education system. However, many argue that this framework has also led to unintended consequences, including the erosion of academic rigor and the rise of social activism within schools. Critics believe that Dewey's emphasis on education as a tool for social reform encouraged teachers to shift their focus away from transmitting core knowledge and toward promoting political ideologies.

The connection between Dewey's philosophy and later Marxist leaning ideas in American education is a significant point of controversy. Dewey's belief in education as a force for social change resonated with many left wing activists, some of whom used his theories as a foundation for promoting socialist ideals in the classroom. The rise of Critical Pedagogy, for example, a teaching philosophy that encourages students to question power structures and fight for social justice can be traced back in part to Dewey's ideas about the role of education in shaping society.

As progressive education gained traction, traditional values and classical learning were increasingly pushed aside. Schools began to emphasize concepts like equality, social justice, and group collaboration ideas that, while not inherently negative, became vehicles for promoting specific political agendas. Dewey's focus on collective learning mirrored socialist ideals, raising concerns that the education system was being used to subtly promote a worldview that undermines individual responsibility and free market principles.

In many ways, the legacy of Dewey's influence can still be seen in today's public schools. From the emphasis on group projects to the push for diversity, equity, and inclusion programs, the modern education system reflects Dewey's vision of using education to shape not only individuals but also society as a whole. Critics argue that this has contributed to the current cultural divide, as schools increasingly prioritize political and social activism over academic excellence and intellectual rigor.

Dewey's impact is not just historical, it is deeply embedded in the very foundation of American education. While some praise him for transforming education into a more dynamic and engaging process. Others warn that his ideas opened the door for the politicization of public schools. They argue that Dewey's sympathy for socialist ideals helped pave the way for later movements that promote Marxist thought under the guise of progressive education.

In sum, John Dewey's role in American education is a story of both innovation and controversy. His ideas revolutionized teaching methods, but they also blurred the line between education and social engineering. Dewey's legacy serves as a reminder that education is never a neutral enterprise, it shapes not only minds but also values, and the direction it takes has profound implications for society. His influence remains a subject of debate, as parents and educators wrestle with the question of what kind of citizens schools are really producing, and what kind of society those citizens will ultimately create.

John Dewey's impact on American education and broader societal values runs deep. Influencing not only teaching practices but also the philosophical underpinnings of how schools engage with students, communities, and political thought. His ideas helped lay the groundwork for public education to shift from a focus on traditional knowledge toward a progressive framework that emphasizes social transformation. While Dewey's ideas were intended to promote democracy, creativity, and experiential learning. They have also been criticized for weakening academic standards, encouraging political activism, and reshaping the role of education in ways that critics argue have contributed to the erosion of American values.

Dewey was one of the primary architects of pragmatism, a philosophy that centers on practical outcomes rather than absolute truths. This philosophical shift was significant because it directly challenged the classical education model, which sought to instill timeless knowledge through the study of history, literature, and moral philosophy. Dewey believed that education should focus not on the mastery of abstract knowledge, but on preparing students to solve real world problems. His approach turned schools into laboratories for social experimentation, where students could learn through experience rather than rote memorization.

While this may seem like a positive development, critics argue that Dewey's focus on pragmatism introduced a relativistic mindset into education. If knowledge is only valued for its practical utility, then the idea of objective truth becomes secondary. This shift opened the door for schools to de-emphasize subjects like history, literature, and civics in favor of more fluid, experiential subjects that reflect the interests of students and the current social environment. Over time, this contributed to what some see as the intellectual decline in public education, with students graduating without a firm grasp of history or critical thinking skills rooted in logical reasoning.

One of the most enduring aspects of Dewey's philosophy was his rejection of rugged individualism, which had long been a cornerstone of American society. Dewey believed that education should encourage students to think of themselves as part of a collective whole rather than as independent actors pursuing their own goals. While his focus on collaboration and social responsibility was intended to strengthen democratic ideals, it also mirrored socialist and collectivist thought. Dewey's model encouraged students to view their personal success as tied to the success of the group, a principle that aligned with the emerging ideas of social reform movements at the time.

This collectivist approach also found its way into how teachers were trained. Teacher education programs inspired by Dewey began to emphasize that educators should act as facilitators of social change rather than merely transmitters of knowledge. The role of the teacher evolved from being an authoritative figure imparting wisdom, to a guide helping students navigate their own learning experiences. Critics argue that this shift undermined discipline and accountability in the classroom. As the focus turned toward nurturing self expression and group dynamics over mastery of content.

Dewey's philosophy also helped shape the way education systems are structured. His ideas about collective learning and social responsibility resonated with the growing teachers' unions of the 20th century, which began to see their role not just as advocates for teachers but as drivers of broader social change. The American Federation of Teachers and the National Education Association both adopted progressive principles in their platforms. Promoting policies that aligned with Dewey's vision of education as a means of achieving equity and social reform. This alignment between unions and progressive education policies has had a lasting effect on the structure of public schools, contributing to the rise of large educational bureaucracies focused on implementing social agendas.

Over time, the bureaucratic model that emerged in American public schools began to prioritize compliance with policies and frameworks. Many of which were based on Dewey's educational philosophy, over actual learning outcomes. Teachers were encouraged to follow set guidelines focused on inclusivity and emotional well being, sometimes at the expense of academic rigor. The result critics argue, has been a system that is more concerned with fostering politically correct environments than with preparing students for higher learning or competitive careers.

Perhaps one of the most controversial aspects of Dewey's legacy is how his philosophy paved the way for political activism to take root in schools. Dewey believed that education should serve as a means of achieving social progress, and this idea has resonated with various social movements throughout the years. His influence is evident in the development of Critical Pedagogy, a teaching philosophy that encourages students to question and challenge existing power structures. Proponents argue that this approach empowers students to become agents of change, but critics warn that it fosters resentment, entitlement, and a focus on grievance politics.

The idea that students should be taught to view themselves as activists rather than scholars has become increasingly prevalent in today's public schools. Teachers are often encouraged to integrate social justice themes into their lessons, promoting ideas that reflect progressive and left wing ideologies. This trend is particularly visible in subjects like history and literature, where traditional narratives have been replaced by frameworks that emphasize systemic oppression and the need for collective action. Critics argue that this approach not only distorts historical facts but also discourages independent thought by promoting conformity to a specific ideological perspective.

Another unintended consequence of Dewey's philosophy is the erosion of academic standards. In his push to create a more student centered learning environment, Dewey de-emphasized the importance of mastering core knowledge and skills. His focus on experiential learning led to the idea that students should learn at their own pace and explore subjects based on personal interests. While this approach can foster creativity and engagement, it has also resulted in a lack of structure and accountability in many classrooms.

Today, many educators and parents express concern that public schools have sacrificed academic rigor in favor of emotional and social development. Standardized test scores have declined, and many students graduate without the skills necessary to succeed in college or the workforce. Critics argue that Dewey's emphasis on self directed learning has created a culture of mediocrity, where students are not challenged to reach their full potential.

In summary, John Dewey's impact on American education is vast and complex. While his ideas brought positive changes, such as making learning more engaging and relevant, they also contributed to the politicization of education and the decline of academic standards. Dewey's progressive philosophy encouraged schools to move away from transmitting objective knowledge and toward promoting social change, a shift that has had far reaching consequences.

Dewey's influence is still felt today, as schools grapple with balancing academic achievement and social agendas. His legacy serves as a cautionary tale about the power of ideas to shape institutions and the unintended consequences that can arise when education is used as a tool for social engineering. The current debates over the role of public education, whether it should focus on academics or activism, can be traced back, in part, to the philosophies Dewey introduced over a century ago.

Elizabeth Bartholet: A Harvard Professor Challenging Homeschooling

Elizabeth Bartholet is a professor at Harvard Law School with a long career focused on civil rights, family law, and child welfare. Throughout her career, Bartholet has been a vocal advocate for children's rights and has drawn attention to issues like adoption and foster care reform. However, she gained widespread attention and controversy for her outspoken criticism of homeschooling in the United States.

Bartholet's opposition to homeschooling centers on her concerns about lack of oversight and regulation. In a 2020 piece published in the Arizona Law Review and later highlighted by Harvard Magazine, Bartholet argued that homeschooling presents risks to children's education and welfare, especially because it allows parents to operate with minimal state intervention. She suggested that homeschooling could lead to educational neglect, social isolation, and in some cases, abuse.

Bartholet further contended that the homeschooling environment may foster authoritarian control by parents and shelter children from exposure to diverse viewpoints. She expressed concern that children educated at home would not develop the critical thinking skills necessary to function in a pluralistic society. As they may not encounter ideas about democracy, equality, and tolerance that are part of public education curricula.

Bartholet's critique particularly targets christian conservative homeschoolers, whom she believes may use homeschooling to shield their children from secular values. She raised concerns about these parents teaching ideas that conflict with mainstream science, such as skepticism toward evolution or progressive social values. Her view is that children should have the opportunity to explore alternative worldviews and not be confined to their parents' ideology.

In one of her more controversial recommendations, Bartholet proposed a "presumptive ban" on homeschooling. Under this policy, parents would need to justify why their children should be homeschooled, and homeschooling would no longer be a default option. She argued that the state has a duty to ensure that all children receive an education that prepares them for participation in a democratic society. Bartholet's proposal would shift the burden onto parents to prove that homeschooling is necessary, rather than allowing it to proceed unchecked.

Bartholet's comments sparked an immediate backlash from homeschooling advocates, educators, and parents. Critics argued that her stance was elitist, dismissive of parental rights, and based on outdated stereotypes. Organizations like the Home School Legal Defense Association pushed back, pointing out that research shows homeschooled children generally perform well academically and socially. They also noted that parents often choose homeschooling not to isolate their children, but to protect them from bullying, indoctrination, or unsafe environments in public schools.

Others accused Bartholet of seeking to impose ideological conformity by forcing children into public education systems that promote progressive values. They argued that her call for government oversight was excessive and would infringe on parents' fundamental rights to direct their children's education and upbringing.

The controversy intensified when Bartholet was slated to host a Harvard summit on homeschooling, which was later postponed due to public criticism and the COVID-19 pandemic. The summit was framed by opponents as an attack on homeschooling, with many seeing Bartholet's stance as part of a broader push to undermine parental authority in favor of state control.

Bartholet's critique of homeschooling has amplified the debate about education, parental rights, and state involvement. While her advocacy has resonated with those concerned about the quality and accountability of homeschooling, it has also galvanized opposition among parents and religious communities who view her proposals as overreach.

Her work reflects a broader cultural divide between those who trust parents to make educational decisions for their children and those who believe the state must play a more active role in ensuring educational standards and protecting children's rights. The impact of Bartholet's advocacy has extended beyond academia, fueling debates about educational freedom, religious liberty, and the role of public schools in shaping societal values.

Ultimately, Elizabeth Bartholet's story underscores the tension between personal freedom and government regulation. Her call for greater oversight of homeschooling may appeal to those who fear educational neglect or abuse, but it has also become a rallying point for defenders of parental rights. Whether her ideas gain traction in future policy debates remains to be seen, but Bartholet's impact on the conversation around homeschooling has already left a lasting mark.

Alexandria Ocasio Cortez: A Meteoric Rise, Wrapped in Ideology

Alexandria Ocasio Cortez, better known as AOC, burst onto the political scene like a social media influencer who stumbled into congress. And, in a way, that's exactly what happened. She went from bartending in New York to becoming the youngest woman ever elected to the U.S. House of Representatives. But don't let her grassroots, "woman of the people" narrative fool you, AOC's story isn't just about shaking up Washington with fresh ideas. It's about how someone can leverage charisma, social media savvy, and radical ideology to become one of the most influential and divisive political figures in the country.

Her rise to fame started when she unseated Joe Crowley, a ten term Democratic incumbent, in the 2018 primary. That was no small feat. Crowley was considered part of the Democratic machine, a major power player, but AOC's victory sent a shockwave through the political establishment. It became clear that the new guard wasn't just looking to tweak policies here and there, they were aiming to overhaul the entire system. The victory wasn't just a win for her campaign, it was a win for a far left ideology that has steadily crept into mainstream politics.

Once in Congress, AOC wasted no time making headlines, proposing policies like the Green New Deal, a sweeping environmental plan that had more to do with social transformation than saving the planet. The deal wasn't just about clean energy, it included provisions for universal healthcare, job guarantees, and even addressed systemic racism. That's right, AOC packaged climate policy with a political wish list that read like a progressive fever dream. Of course, when pressed on how to pay for it, her response was simple, "You just do." Apparently, balancing budgets is an outdated concept when your solution is to print more money.

What's remarkable about AOC's story isn't just her rise to power but how she became the voice of a movement by weaponizing media and outrage. She mastered the art of soundbites quick. Catchy phrases designed to go viral and turned social media into her personal bullhorn. When criticized, she painted herself as the perpetual underdog, the young Latina woman battling the establishment and the forces of oppression. It was a brilliant strategy. Any disagreement with her was framed as an attack on her identity or proof that the critic was out of touch with the modern world.

AOC's story also illustrates the power of identity politics in modern American culture. She didn't just present policies, she presented herself as a symbol of progress. And in today's political climate, symbolism is often more important than substance. Her ability to cast herself as a champion for marginalized communities has given her a loyal following, but it's also alienated a large swath of the population who see through the rhetoric.

In many ways, AOC's story is about the shift from governing to branding. She treats every policy debate like a social media post, designed not to persuade but to galvanize. Whether she's showing off her $58 "Tax the Rich" dress at a Met Gala attended by billionaires or live streaming from her apartment, AOC blurs the lines between activism and theater. She's not just a politician, she's a performance artist.

And that's the real kicker. Her policies, however impractical or outlandish they may seem, aren't meant to pass. They're meant to shift the Overton window, to make the once unthinkable sound almost reasonable by comparison. Sure, we might not pass the Green New Deal tomorrow, but if we move a little closer to government controlled everything? Mission accomplished.

AOC's story is the story of modern American politics, part spectacle, part ideology, and part social media masterclass. She's not just challenging the system, she's reshaping it in her image. Whether that's a good thing or a dangerous one depends on who you ask. But one thing's for sure, AOC's rise proves that in today's world, it's not about having good ideas. It's about being able to sell them.

AOC's impact isn't just in the policies she proposes, most of which are more symbolic than realistic, but in how she has fundamentally changed the tone, priorities, and even the methods of American politics. Love her or hate her, Alexandria Ocasio Cortez has altered the game, moving the Democratic Party, and by extension, the national political discourse, further to the left than it has been in decades.

One of the biggest impacts of AOC is how she's normalized the once fringe idea of socialism. A generation ago, the word "socialism" was politically toxic, something politicians avoided at all costs. Now, thanks to AOC and her allies in the progressive "Squad," it's practically a rallying cry. Through policies like the Green New Deal and Medicare for All, AOC has rebranded socialism as "democratic socialism," which she insists is merely about fairness and equity. But in practice, it's about vastly expanding the role of government in every corner of life from healthcare to energy to housing.

AOC's Green New Deal may not have passed, but that wasn't the point. The real point was to drag the Overton window to the left. Policies that once seemed radical, like government funded healthcare or guaranteed jobs, now dominate the political conversation. By proposing policies that are extreme, AOC has made slightly less extreme ideas seem reasonable by comparison. Even when her legislation fails, she wins by shifting the narrative. Now, mainstream Democrats are debating the degree of government expansion, not whether it should expand at all.

Her influence extends far beyond Congress. Through her social media presence, AOC has inspired a generation of activists to see politics as a form of cultural warfare. She's made it clear that political engagement isn't just about passing laws, it's about controlling the narrative. Every Instagram live, every viral tweet, is part of her broader strategy to shape public opinion and galvanize her base. AOC understands that in the modern world, politics is as much about theater as it is about governance, and she's mastered the art of both.

Her impact can also be seen in the Democratic Party's shift toward identity politics. AOC has turned personal identity into a political weapon, reframing criticism of her policies as attacks on her race, gender, or background. This tactic not only shields her from scrutiny but also changes the nature of political debate. Instead of arguing over policy details, debates now revolve around identity and perception. Her supporters see her as the embodiment of progress. A young Latina woman fighting against a corrupt system while her critics argue that her reliance on identity politics stifles meaningful discussion and divides the nation further.

One of the most profound and for many, troubling impacts of AOC's rise is the normalization of grievance based politics. Her rhetoric often focuses on systemic oppression, inequality, and victimhood, framing society as a battle between the oppressed and the oppressors. This has fueled a culture where individuals are encouraged to view themselves primarily through the lens of victimization, blaming external systems rather than personal responsibility for their challenges. AOC's speeches and social media posts reinforce this mindset, encouraging young people to see government intervention as the primary solution to personal and societal problems.

Another key impact of AOC is the rise of cancel culture within political discourse. AOC has shown that public figures who don't align with the progressive agenda can be shamed, silenced, or ostracized. Whether she's calling for boycotts, criticizing fellow Democrats, or attacking political opponents, AOC wields social media outrage like a weapon. Her style of politics promotes a zero tolerance approach to disagreement, where dissent isn't debated, it's canceled.

Her influence also extends to environmental policy. While the Green New Deal failed legislatively, it succeeded culturally. Many cities and states have adopted climate goals inspired by its framework, and mainstream politicians now speak in terms of climate "justice" rather than just environmentalism. Even companies have begun adopting the language of AOC's climate agenda, implementing sustainability goals more out of political pressure than practical necessity.

Perhaps most concerning is the generational shift AOC has fostered. Younger voters now see her and the policies she promotes not as radical, but as common sense. Concepts like government funded housing, free college, and open borders are embraced with little thought given to the long term consequences. AOC has successfully tapped into the frustrations of younger generations, particularly those saddled with student debt and job instability, promising them a future where government takes care of their needs. While these promises are appealing, they also carry significant risks, as they assume the government can solve complex societal problems through simple solutions, something history repeatedly warns against.

AOC's impact on the relationship between politicians and their constituents has also shifted dramatically. By bypassing traditional media and engaging directly with her audience through social media, AOC has made politics more personal and immediate. She's created a model where politicians are expected to constantly engage with the public, blurring the line between public servant and influencer. This shift has increased transparency, but it has also made politics more reactive, driven by the latest viral moment rather than thoughtful policy debate.

In summary, AOC's impact on American politics is profound. She's shifted the Democratic Party to the left, normalized socialism, reshaped political debate through identity politics, and inspired a generation to view government as the solution to all problems. Her ability to control the narrative and galvanize her base through social media has made her one of the most influential politicians of our time, even though many of her legislative efforts have failed. AOC's impact is less about what she has accomplished directly and more about the cultural shift she has engineered. A shift that has redefined the nature of political engagement and set the stage for a future where ideological activism dominates the political landscape.

The Rise of Gavin Newsom: A Charismatic Politician with Lofty Ambitions

Gavin Newsom's political story is one of ambition, charisma, and controversy. He's been a rising star in the Democratic Party for years, positioning himself as a progressive leader with an eye on shaping California and perhaps the nation into a model for liberal governance. But behind the polished image and slick speeches lies a complex tale of contradictions, policy misfires, and deepening divisions under his watch.

Newsom's rise began in San Francisco, where he served as mayor from 2004 to 2011. During his time as mayor, Newsom made national headlines by issuing marriage licenses to same sex couples, defying state law at the time. It was a bold move that garnered him both praise and condemnation, but it cemented his reputation as a progressive trailblazer willing to push boundaries. For Newsom, it wasn't just about policy, it was about making a statement. And that's been the defining characteristic of his political style ever since. Grand gestures, sweeping rhetoric, and promises of transformative change.

From there, Newsom's political star only continued to rise. He was elected lieutenant governor of California in 2011 and later ascended to the governorship in 2019. As governor, he vowed to tackle California's biggest challenges housing, climate change, homelessness, and healthcare with bold, progressive policies. But while his speeches painted a utopian vision, the reality of his tenure has been anything but.

One of the biggest controversies of Newsom's leadership has been his handling of the homelessness crisis. Despite pouring billions of dollars into programs to address homelessness, the problem has only worsened under his watch. Tent cities have sprung up across California's major urban centers, and residents both housed and unhoused, find themselves trapped in an increasingly dysfunctional system. Critics argue that Newsom's policies, which focus heavily on temporary shelters and harm reduction strategies, have only enabled the problem rather than solving it. But Newsom dismisses such criticism, often framing homelessness as a symptom of national inequality rather than his administration's failure.

Then came the COVID-19 pandemic, a crisis that would define Newsom's governorship. In the early days of the pandemic, Newsom imposed some of the strictest lockdown measures in the country, including extended business closures and school shutdowns. He touted California as a model for pandemic management, but his handling of the crisis soon sparked outrage. Parents grew frustrated as schools remained closed for months, businesses shuttered, and millions of Californians were pushed into unemployment. Meanwhile, private schools reopened long before public ones, and wealthy residents simply left the state. The middle class, trapped under the weight of rising costs and declining opportunities, began to question whether Newsom's California was a place they could continue to call home.

The breaking point for many came when Newsom was caught dining at the exclusive French Laundry restaurant maskless, while telling Californians to stay home. It wasn't just the hypocrisy that angered people, it was the fact that this dinner took place at the height of the pandemic restrictions, rubbing salt in the wound for residents who had lost businesses, jobs, and even loved ones. Newsom later apologized, but the damage was done. The incident became a symbol of the double standards and elitism many critics believe define his leadership.

Amid growing frustrations, Newsom faced a recall effort in 2021, the second governor in California's history to do so. While he survived the recall with the help of a massive campaign and national Democratic support, the episode exposed the deep cracks in California's political landscape. Newsom's opponents criticized him for failing to address the state's crises. Homelessness, wildfires, crime, and skyrocketing living costs, while his supporters framed the recall as a partisan attack from far right extremists. Newsom emerged victorious, but the recall revealed the growing disconnect between his administration and the frustrations of ordinary Californians.

Newsom's leadership style relies heavily on grand narratives about California's potential to be a beacon of progressive values. He has championed environmental policies like banning the sale of new gasoline powered cars by 2035 and expanding the use of renewable energy. But his critics argue that these ambitious goals are often more performative than practical. California's electric grid, for example, has struggled to keep up with demand during heatwaves, resulting in rolling blackouts, raising the question of whether the state's push toward green energy is outpacing its infrastructure.

Meanwhile, crime rates in California have surged, further straining Newsom's relationship with residents. His approach to criminal justice reform focused on reducing incarceration and shifting funds from policing to social programs has drawn criticism from law enforcement and communities alike. As violent crime rises, many Californians feel less safe, and Newsom's policies are increasingly blamed for fostering an environment where lawlessness is tolerated.

Yet despite these challenges, Newsom remains a force in American politics. He's cultivated a national profile, positioning himself as a defender of progressive ideals and a potential future presidential candidate. He regularly sparrs with red state governors like Florida's Ron DeSantis, portraying himself as the antidote to conservative policies and a champion of equality and inclusion. Newsom's critics see these national ambitions as a distraction from California's deepening crises, arguing that he's more interested in building his brand than fixing the problems at home.

In the end, Gavin Newsom's story is one of contrasts. He promises transformation but struggles to deliver results. He champions equality while dining with elites. He frames himself as a progressive hero but faces growing disillusionment from those he governs. Newsom's impact extends beyond policy, it's about how he represents the future of the progressive movement. For better or worse, his leadership reflects the challenges and contradictions of modern liberal governance, where bold rhetoric often collides with the harsh realities of governing a deeply divided state.

Gavin Newsom's impact extends well beyond California's borders, offering both a model and a cautionary tale of progressive governance. His policies reflect a vision of a future shaped by environmental mandates, criminal justice reform, social equality initiatives, and ambitious government expansion. However, Newsom's impact has not been without severe consequences, many of which expose the limits of idealism when faced with economic, social, and political realities.

One of Newsom's most well known legacies is his aggressive push for green energy. His administration set the ambitious goal of banning the sale of new gas powered vehicles by 2035, aiming to position California as a global leader in environmental policy. While the goal appeals to climate activists, critics argue that it's disconnected from the practical realities faced by ordinary Californians.

California's energy infrastructure, under Newsom's leadership, has struggled to keep pace with the push for electrification. Rolling blackouts have become a familiar summer occurrence, leaving residents and businesses in the dark during peak demand. This has raised questions about whether the state's energy grid can support the influx of electric vehicles and renewable energy mandates. Critics see this as a prime example of Newsom's tendency to make grand promises without fully addressing the logistical and economic challenges that follow.

Beyond the energy sector, Newsom's environmental policies have contributed to the growing cost of living. Gas prices in California are among the highest in the nation, thanks in part to environmental taxes and regulations. While Newsom insists these sacrifices are necessary to combat climate change, they have placed a disproportionate burden on working class families, many of whom are already struggling with the state's high cost of housing and everyday expenses.

Under Newsom's tenure, California's homelessness crisis has reached unprecedented levels. Billions of dollars have been allocated to address the issue, but the results have been dismal. Tent cities have sprung up in major urban centers like Los Angeles, San Francisco, and Oakland, with little improvement despite increased funding. Newsom's policies, which focus on providing temporary housing and harm reduction strategies rather than addressing the root causes of homelessness, have been widely criticized for enabling, rather than alleviating, the problem.

Newsom's impact on public safety has been equally contentious. His administration has pushed for criminal justice reforms that emphasize decarceration and reducing the role of law enforcement. While these reforms are framed as steps toward equity and fairness, the reality has been a surge in crime. Theft, assault, and property crime rates have skyrocketed, with businesses and residents feeling the effects. Retail theft has become so rampant that major retailers have begun closing stores in San Francisco and other cities, citing crime as the primary reason.

Residents and law enforcement officials argue that Newsom's policies have emboldened criminals and demoralized police. The emphasis on decriminalizing non violent offenses and reducing sentences has, in practice, created a perception of lawlessness. For many Californians, especially in urban areas, the erosion of public safety has become a defining issue of Newsom's leadership.

The economic impact of Newsom's governance has been profound, especially on California's middle class. Between the soaring cost of living, increasing taxes, and the state's regulatory burden, many middle class families have found it increasingly difficult to stay afloat. Newsom's California has become a place where only the very wealthy and the very poor can survive. One benefits from the system, and the other is supported by it. The middle class, caught between high taxes and skyrocketing costs, has been fleeing the state in droves.

In fact, California has experienced a population decline for the first time in its history, with families and businesses leaving for states with lower taxes and more affordable living conditions. States like Texas and Florida have become popular destinations for Californians seeking relief from the financial strain and regulatory overreach that Newsom's policies have created. While Newsom dismisses the exodus as politically motivated, the loss of taxpayers and businesses has put additional strain on the state's finances, threatening its ability to maintain the very social programs he champions.

Newsom's impact on education has also drawn significant criticism. Under his administration, public schools were among the last to reopen during the COVID-19 pandemic, even as private schools and schools in other states resumed in person learning. Parents became increasingly frustrated as they watched their children fall behind academically, with mental health issues on the rise due to prolonged isolation.

Despite the evidence that schools could reopen safely, Newsom sided with teachers' unions, which lobbied for extended closures and additional funding. This decision had long term consequences for students, particularly those from low income families, who now face widening achievement gaps and declining academic performance. Parents have grown disillusioned with the public education system, leading to an increase in homeschooling and private school enrollment.

Newsom's support for progressive curricula, including the promotion of critical race theory and gender ideology, has further alienated parents. Many feel that the state's education policies are more focused on social engineering than academic excellence. The disconnect between parents and public institutions has fueled a growing distrust in the state government, with many families feeling that their values are no longer represented in California's public schools.

Despite the controversies and crises in California, Newsom has emerged as a prominent national figure, positioning himself as a potential future presidential candidate. He has framed California as a model for progressive governance, arguing that the state's environmental policies, social programs, and equity initiatives represent the future of the country. Newsom frequently engages in public spats with conservative governors like Ron DeSantis. Using these confrontations to position himself as the champion of progressive values on the national stage.

However, Newsom's national influence is a double edged sword. While he has become a hero to the progressive left, his leadership has also served as a warning for other states. Critics argue that California's problems, crime, homelessness, high taxes, and declining public services, are the direct result of policies that prioritize ideology over practicality. As other states watch California's struggles, many have become wary of adopting similar policies, seeing Newsom's governance as a cautionary tale rather than a blueprint for success.

Gavin Newsom's impact is defined by contradictions. He promises transformation but struggles to deliver meaningful change. He champions environmentalism while presiding over blackouts. He advocates for equity while overseeing the decline of public services. His policies, while ambitious in scope, often fail to address the complexities of real world governance, leaving Californians to bear the brunt of his ideological pursuits.

At the same time, Newsom's influence extends beyond policy. He represents a new style of leadership, where politics is as much about performance and narrative as it is about results. Newsom's ability to control the narrative, framing every criticism as a partisan attack and every failure as a necessary sacrifice for progress has allowed him to maintain his political standing even as California faces mounting challenges.

In the end, Gavin Newsom's impact is a testament to the power of ideology in shaping governance. His leadership offers both a vision of what progressive governance can achieve and a warning about its unintended consequences. As California continues to grapple with the fallout of his policies, Newsom's legacy will serve as a case study in the complexities of balancing idealism with reality.

Alyssa Milano: The Celebrity Activist Who Made Abortion Her Platform

Alyssa Milano's story is a prime example of how cultural influence has shifted from traditional values to activism that promotes narratives in direct conflict with christian teachings. Milano, best known for her roles in TV shows like Who's the Boss? and Charmed, has used her celebrity status to amplify progressive causes, most notably abortion rights. Her public activism has become a case study in how Hollywood elites push controversial agendas, often alienating those with differing beliefs while shaping public policy debates through social media and cultural clout.

Milano's transformation from actress to activist gained national attention in 2019, during a heated national conversation surrounding the passage of restrictive abortion laws, particularly Georgia's "heartbeat bill." The bill aimed to ban abortions after the detection of a fetal heartbeat, which typically occurs around six weeks of pregnancy. Rather than engaging in nuanced debate, Milano responded with a call for a sex strike, urging women to withhold sex until reproductive rights were secured. This strategy, which she framed as empowering, was widely mocked for being reductive and tone deaf, but it accomplished what Milano intended, it got her attention.

In a viral tweet, Milano called her two abortions in the 1990s the "right decision" for her at the time, saying they allowed her to pursue her career and personal goals. For Milano, the act of ending a pregnancy was not seen as a tragic necessity but as a path to personal freedom, a narrative that directly conflicts with christian values that view life as sacred from conception.

Milano's rhetoric has also played a significant role in normalizing abortion. Through her podcasts, television appearances, and relentless social media activism, she has promoted the idea that abortion is a moral good, something to be celebrated, not regretted. Her message is clear, women cannot be truly free unless they have the power to terminate pregnancies without restriction. In this sense, Milano's activism ties directly into the broader cultural shift toward moral relativism, where individual choice is placed above all else, even the sanctity of life.

But Milano's advocacy doesn't stop with abortion. She has become a leading voice in Hollywood's opposition to pro life legislation, calling for boycotts of states that pass restrictive abortion laws. She led efforts to pressure film studios to pull production out of Georgia, where many companies had taken advantage of generous tax incentives, arguing that the state's heartbeat bill was an attack on women's rights. Her activism sparked a broader conversation about corporate responsibility and the growing influence of Hollywood in shaping public policy.

Milano's activism also highlights a troubling trend. The growing divide between those who view morality as defined by Scripture and those who see it as fluid and subject to personal preference. Her unapologetic defense of abortion as a means of personal empowerment embodies the cultural shift that has taken place over the past few decades, where the pursuit of personal freedom is placed above all other values. Her story serves as a reminder of the consequences of the church's silence. When the church fails to speak out, voices like Milano's fill the void, shaping public opinion and policy in ways that further erode the moral fabric of society.

In many ways, Milano's activism reveals the battle being waged for the soul of the nation. It's not just a political fight, it's a cultural and spiritual one. Figures like Milano have mastered the art of using emotion and personal narrative to sway public opinion, leaving the church struggling to keep up. While she frames her advocacy as a fight for justice and equality, it's clear that her message is rooted in a worldview that places human autonomy above God's design for life and family.

Ultimately, Alyssa Milano's story underscores the urgency of the church's role in engaging with culture. The silence from the pulpit has allowed activists like her to define the narrative, leaving christians on the defensive. If the church continues to remain passive, voices like Milano's will only grow louder, further entrenching ideas that are antithetical to the gospel and destructive to society.

Alyssa Milano's activism represents more than just an individual's personal journey, it's part of a broader cultural shift where celebrities wield significant influence over public opinion, policy, and moral values. Her advocacy for abortion rights, in particular, has contributed to the normalization of abortion as a form of empowerment and a right that defines modern womanhood. Her impact is felt across media, politics, and the entertainment industry, as well as in the cultural clash between secularism and christianity.

Milano's decision to publicly frame abortion as an empowering choice for women has had a profound impact on the public narrative surrounding the issue. Her personal testimony, candidly discussing her two abortions as necessary for her personal, and career development contributes to the growing trend of viewing abortion not just as a difficult choice but as a positive good. This narrative, promoted through her public appearances and social media platforms, aligns with a cultural message that prioritizes personal freedom and career success over the sanctity of life.

Milano's story reinforces the idea that motherhood and professional ambition are mutually exclusive, a message that has been amplified in feminist circles. For young women and girls, this narrative promotes the belief that achieving personal goals must come at the expense of family life, subtly teaching them that children are obstacles rather than blessings. This mindset is a direct challenge to biblical teachings about the value of life and the importance of family. Her voice has effectively reshaped the cultural conversation, normalizing abortion in ways that influence not only individual choices but also public policy.

Milano's activism exemplifies how Hollywood and the entertainment industry have become powerful tools in shaping political discourse. Her call to boycott Georgia over its heartbeat bill highlights the ability of celebrities to rally financial and political pressure against states that adopt conservative policies. Milano's success in mobilizing studios, actors, and activists against pro life legislation demonstrates how cultural elites can influence corporate decisions and public policy. This dynamic raises the stakes for state governments that wish to implement pro-life policies, as they must now contend with financial boycotts and negative media campaigns orchestrated by celebrities like Milano.

The success of these boycotts underscores the challenge faced by the church and pro life advocates. The opposition isn't just political, it's cultural, emotional, and deeply entrenched in media narratives. Milano's role in these campaigns reflects the entertainment industry's shift from neutral storytelling to explicit political activism, with Hollywood becoming an engine for progressive change.

Milano's mastery of social media as a tool for activism has further expanded her influence. Platforms like Twitter and Instagram allow her to bypass traditional media and speak directly to millions of followers, amplifying the pro abortion message in ways that resonate with younger audiences. This direct connection has made her an influential figure among Millennials and Gen Z, normalizing abortion and progressive social values as integral to modern identity.

Her use of personal storieslike the decision to have abortions, serves as a powerful emotional appeal that resonates more than statistics or policy arguments. Milano's ability to blend personal narrative with political activism has become a model for modern advocacy, where the goal is not just to win debates but to change hearts and minds by appealing to emotions. This tactic has proven effective, making it harder for opponents to push back without being labeled as judgmental or out of touch.

Milano's activism has also emboldened the corporate world to take a more active role in shaping public policy. Her campaign against Georgia's heartbeat bill encouraged film studios to threaten to pull production from the state, setting a precedent for corporate activism against conservative legislation. This new dynamic where businesses take sides on moral and political issues has further divided the nation, making it increasingly difficult for individuals and institutions to remain neutral.

For conservative states and christian communities, this trend presents a significant challenge. When corporations align with activists like Milano, it creates economic pressure that discourages the adoption of policies rooted in biblical values. This dynamic underscores the growing influence of cultural elites in shaping not only public opinion but also the legislative landscape, often at the expense of traditional morality.

Milano's impact also reflects the consequences of the church's silence on key moral issues. Her voice has filled the void left by christian leaders who have avoided engaging in cultural debates, either out of fear of backlash or a misguided belief that such matters are "political" rather than spiritual. Milano's success in framing abortion as a human right illustrates what happens when the church steps back from the cultural conversation, alternative narratives take root, and society drifts further from biblical principles.

Her story highlights a broader trend where secular voices dominate the conversation around life, family, and morality, while the church is relegated to the sidelines. In many ways, Milano's activism is a testament to what happens when the church fails to fulfill its role as a moral compass. Without a strong, unified voice from the church, figures like Milano are free to shape public values and policies according to secular ideologies.

Milano's activism has contributed to the growing divide in America over issues like abortion and religious freedom. Her framing of the debate in terms of personal autonomy and women's rights leaves little room for compromise, deepening the cultural rift between those who see life as sacred and those who view it as secondary to individual choice. This division is not just political, it's moral and spiritual, reflecting the deeper conflict between secularism and christianity that defines much of today's cultural landscape.

Her story illustrates how cultural influence, when left unchecked by christian values, can reshape society in ways that are difficult to reverse. As more celebrities and influencers follow Milano's lead, promoting progressive values under the guise of empowerment and equality, the church faces an uphill battle to reclaim its voice in the public square.

Alyssa Milano's impact extends far beyond the entertainment industry. She has become a key figure in the pro abortion movement, using her platform to normalize abortion, promote progressive values, and pressure corporations and governments into aligning with her agenda. Her ability to blend personal narrative with political activism has reshaped the cultural conversation, leaving those who hold traditional christian values struggling to make their voices heard.

Ultimately, Milano's story serves as both a warning and a challenge for the church. It shows how cultural power can be wielded to reshape public values, and it underscores the importance of engaging in cultural debates before alternative narratives become entrenched. Her activism has exposed the consequences of the church's silence, making it clear that if christians don't speak out others will, often with messages that lead society further away from God's design.

Rachel Levine: A Symbol of Cultural Shift and Controversy in American Policy

Rachel Levine's story is emblematic of the rapid cultural shifts taking place in America regarding gender identity and healthcare policy. Levine, a transgender woman and the first openly transgender person confirmed to a federal position by the U.S. Senate, serves as the Assistant Secretary for Health in the Department of Health and Human Services. Her rise to prominence is seen by many as a historic victory for LGBTQ representation, but it has also sparked significant controversy, especially among those who oppose the promotion of gender ideology in public policy and healthcare.

Before joining the Biden administration, Levine was Pennsylvania's Secretary of Health, where she oversaw the state's public health policies during the COVID-19 pandemic. During that time, Levine made headlines for both her management of the pandemic and her personal advocacy for transgender healthcare. One of the more controversial aspects of her tenure in Pennsylvania was a policy that required nursing homes to accept COVID-19 patients, which critics argue contributed to the high death toll in long term care facilities. Adding fuel to the fire, Levine's own mother was quietly moved out of a care facility during this time, an action that many saw as hypocritical and emblematic of the double standards often attributed to political elites.

Despite this controversy, Levine's appointment to the federal government was framed by the Biden administration as a triumph for diversity and inclusion. For her supporters, Levine's rise represents progress toward greater acceptance and equality for marginalized groups. However, her appointment has also drawn sharp criticism from conservatives and christians who view her advocacy for gender affirming care as dangerous, particularly when applied to children.

Levine's most controversial impact lies in her staunch support for gender affirming treatments, including puberty blockers, hormone therapy, and even surgeries for minors experiencing gender dysphoria. She has been an outspoken advocate for removing barriers to these treatments, arguing that such interventions are essential for the mental health and well being of transgender youth. Levine has framed opposition to these treatments as discriminatory, dismissing concerns from parents and medical professionals as rooted in prejudice rather than science.

Critics argue that Levine's stance promotes irreversible medical interventions for children who may not fully understand the long term consequences of their decisions. Many doctors and researchers have warned that puberty blockers and cross sex hormones can cause permanent changes, including infertility, bone density loss, and developmental issues. Yet, Levine insists that these treatments are "life saving" and must be made available without delay, often without requiring parental consent. This position has placed her at the center of one of the most contentious debates in modern healthcare.

Levine's advocacy extends beyond healthcare policy into education, where she has supported efforts to introduce gender identity education in schools. Her endorsement of policies that allow students to socially transition, changing their names and pronouns without notifying parents has fueled concerns about the erosion of parental rights. School districts across the country, inspired by such policies, have implemented guidelines that encourage teachers to affirm a student's gender identity without consulting parents, creating a deep rift between public institutions and families.

In many ways, Levine's story reflects the broader cultural divide between those who embrace progressive values around gender identity and those who hold to traditional views rooted in biology and faith. For christians and conservatives, Levine's promotion of gender ideology represents a direct challenge to biblical teachings about the nature of humanity and God's design for male and female. Her policies are seen not just as misguided but as actively harmful, particularly to vulnerable children who may be pushed into making life altering decisions before they are ready.

Levine's role in the federal government has amplified these concerns, as her influence extends into national policy. Under her leadership, HHS has promoted initiatives to expand access to gender affirming care, including protections that would make it illegal to deny these treatments based on religious or moral objections. For many christians, this encroachment on religious freedom is a sobering reminder of how quickly cultural values can shift when the church fails to engage with the issues of the day.

Levine's advocacy also highlights the power of narrative in shaping public opinion. By framing gender affirming care as essential healthcare and portraying opponents as hateful or ignorant, Levine has successfully shifted the conversation, making it increasingly difficult for dissenting voices to be heard. Media outlets and institutions that challenge this narrative risk being labeled as intolerant or bigoted, further marginalizing those who hold traditional beliefs about gender and sexuality.

Ultimately, Rachel Levine's rise to power is a reminder of the importance of vigilance and the cost of inaction. Her policies represent a profound shift in how society views gender, identity, and healthcare, one that challenges the very foundations of christian belief. Without a strong, unified response from the church, figures like Levine will continue to shape the future, often at the expense of biblical truth and the well being of children.

A deeper look into Rachel Levine's impact reveals how she has become a central figure in advancing gender affirming care policies, often amid significant controversy. Levine's tenure as Assistant Secretary for Health has placed her at the heart of some of the most contentious debates in public health, particularly concerning gender transition treatments for minors.

One key episode involved Levine's reported pressure on the World Professional Association for Transgender Health. To modify its guidelines on pediatric gender transition care. Initially, WPATH had proposed maintaining age limits on certain medical interventions for children, but following Levine's intervention, these restrictions were removed, despite internal concerns about the lack of sufficient scientific backing. The decision underscored the growing politicization of medical guidelines, with critics arguing that this shift prioritizes ideology over evidence based care.

Levine's advocacy extends beyond policy guidelines and into active efforts to push back against state level legislation restricting gender affirming care. She has publicly criticized these laws as harmful to transgender youth, framing them as politically motivated attacks that could lead to increased mental health issues and even suicide within the LGBTQ community. During public appearances, including speeches at events like the Out For Health Conference, Levine emphasized that medical professionals must take a vocal stance against these legislative efforts, further blending public health with advocacy.

Levine's impact is felt not only in policy circles but also in the broader cultural shift toward accepting gender ideology as mainstream. Her story reflects the rapid transformation of public institutions, where policies surrounding gender identity are now positioned as essential aspects of healthcare and civil rights. However, this approach has drawn criticism from parents, medical professionals, and legislators who argue that it undermines parental rights and introduces irreversible medical treatments to vulnerable minors.

In essence, Levine's advocacy is a powerful example of the intersection between public health, politics, and culture. Her push for expanded gender affirming care illustrates how swiftly social ideologies can influence policy, particularly when public opposition is minimal. Her efforts are viewed by some as groundbreaking and by others as a dangerous overreach, encapsulating the deep divisions that now define the conversation around gender and healthcare.

Bill Gates: From Tech Mogul to Global Philanthropist and Controversial Power Player

Bill Gates's story is one of remarkable transformation from the founder of Microsoft and one of the wealthiest individuals in the world to a leading philanthropist and advocate for global health initiatives. But beyond his public persona as a problem solver and innovator, Gates has become a polarizing figure. His initiatives, while ambitious and far reaching, have sparked concerns about the growing influence of private wealth over public policy, especially in areas like education, health, and environmental policy.

After stepping down from his role at Microsoft, Gates shifted his focus to philanthropy through the Bill & Melinda Gates Foundation. The foundation, one of the largest private charitable organizations in the world, directs billions of dollars toward efforts to combat infectious diseases, improve education, and promote sustainable agriculture. Gates's goal has been to harness innovation to address some of the world's most pressing problems, particularly in developing countries. His campaigns to eradicate diseases like malaria and polio have saved millions of lives, earning him international acclaim.

However, Gates's growing influence over public health policies has not come without controversy. His foundation has been instrumental in funding global vaccination programs, and during the COVID-19 pandemic, Gates became a leading voice in promoting vaccines. But this prominence also placed him at the center of conspiracy theories, with some critics accusing him of using health initiatives to exert control over governments and populations. His advocacy for vaccine passports and global health surveillance programs sparked further debate about the balance between public safety and personal freedom.

Gates's impact extends beyond health into education, where he has advocated for reforms based on data driven metrics. His foundation was heavily involved in the promotion of Common Core standards in American schools. While intended to improve educational outcomes, the initiative faced resistance from parents and educators who felt it undermined local control and narrowed the curriculum. The pushback against Common Core highlighted the challenges of top down reform efforts, even when driven by seemingly good intentions.

Another area where Gates has made waves is climate policy. Through his investments in renewable energy technologies and initiatives to combat climate change, Gates has called for a shift away from fossil fuels and a move toward sustainable development. In his book How to Avoid a Climate Disaster, Gates lays out a roadmap for reducing greenhouse gas emissions to zero. However, critics argue that his investments in experimental technologies and reliance on carbon offsets reflect a technocratic approach that may not adequately address the complexities of the climate crisis.

Perhaps the most contentious aspect of Gates's story is the power dynamic his philanthropy creates. The sheer scale of his wealth and the influence of the Gates Foundation have raised questions about accountability. When private individuals wield as much power as governments, critics argue, it blurs the lines between philanthropy and policy making. Gates's efforts, while undeniably impactful, exemplify how private wealth can shape public agendas, sometimes without the transparency and oversight expected of public institutions.

Gates's story is a testament to the transformative power of wealth and innovation, but it also serves as a cautionary tale about the concentration of power. His influence spans across industries, affecting health, education, climate, and technology. For some, he is a visionary who uses his resources to tackle humanity's greatest challenges. For others, he represents the dangers of unchecked influence, where private wealth drives public policy in ways that may not always align with the best interests of society.

Bill Gates's impact spans multiple sectors, public health, education, and climate policy, leaving a lasting, though controversial, mark on the world. Through the Bill & Melinda Gates Foundation, Gates has leveraged his immense wealth to influence policies, fund initiatives, and shape global agendas, making him one of the most powerful private individuals in the modern era. However, his unprecedented influence has also raised concerns about accountability, transparency, and the consequences of concentrating so much power in private hands.

The Gates Foundation has been instrumental in funding vaccination campaigns and disease eradication efforts worldwide. Its programs to combat malaria, polio, and other infectious diseases have saved millions of lives, especially in developing countries. Gates's leadership in promoting COVID-19 vaccination further cemented his role as a global health authority. He personally invested in vaccine research and urged wealthy nations to share doses with poorer countries, framing vaccine distribution as a moral imperative.

Despite these achievements, Gates's involvement in public health has not been without controversy. His support for global health surveillance programs and vaccine passports during the COVID-19 pandemic sparked fierce debate about personal freedoms versus public safety. Moreover, critics argue that Gates's top down approach to health policy can undermine local governments and organizations. For instance, some African leaders have expressed concerns that the focus on Western driven vaccination programs neglects other pressing public health issues that don't align with Gates's priorities.

His advocacy for intellectual property protections during the pandemic also drew backlash. While Gates argued that maintaining patent protections would ensure quality control. Activists and governments in developing countries accused him of prioritizing pharmaceutical profits over global health equity. The refusal to temporarily waive patents on COVID-19 vaccines intensified debates about inequality in global health governance.

Gates has also left a significant mark on education policy, particularly in the United States. His foundation was a leading force behind the Common Core standards, an initiative designed to improve student outcomes through standardized curriculum and assessments. While Common Core was intended to reduce educational disparities, it faced widespread opposition from parents and teachers who felt it imposed rigid teaching methods and stripped local communities of control over their schools.

The backlash against Common Core highlighted the challenges of implementing large scale reforms driven by private philanthropists. Critics argue that Gates underestimated the complexity of the American education system and over relied on data driven metrics at the expense of individual student needs. Although the foundation has since pivoted away from directly funding Common Core, the initiative left a legacy of frustration and division in the education community.

Beyond Common Core, the Gates Foundation continues to influence education by funding charter schools and teacher evaluation systems tied to student performance. These efforts reflect Gates's belief in innovation and accountability, but they have also fueled debates about the privatization of education and the role of wealthy individuals in shaping public policy.

Gates's involvement in climate policy reflects his belief that technological innovation is key to solving the "so called" climate crisis. Through investments in renewable energy, electric vehicles, and carbon capture technology, Gates has promoted a vision of a future where technology mitigates the worst effects of climate change. His 2021 book, How to Avoid a Climate Disaster, outlines a roadmap for achieving net zero emissions by 2050.

However, Gates's approach to climate change has drawn criticism for being overly focused on technological solutions while downplaying the need for systemic economic changes. Activists argue that his investments in carbon offsets allow corporations to continue polluting while claiming environmental responsibility. Gates's heavy reliance on experimental technologies, such as geoengineering, raises ethical questions about unintended consequences and the potential risks of manipulating the planet's climate systems.

Additionally, Gates's personal lifestyle has come under scrutiny. Despite his public advocacy for reducing carbon emissions, he owns multiple homes, private jets, and other luxury assets with large carbon footprints. This perceived hypocrisy has led critics to question whether Gates's environmental agenda is more about controlling the narrative than making meaningful changes.

Perhaps the most significant impact of Gates's philanthropy is the way it has blurred the lines between private wealth and public policy. The Gates Foundation operates on a scale that rivals many governments, raising concerns about accountability and transparency. Unlike elected officials, Gates and his foundation are not subject to public oversight, yet they exert significant influence over global health, education, and environmental policies.

Critics argue that this concentration of power creates a form of "philanthrocapitalism," where wealthy individuals use charitable giving to advance their personal agendas. While Gates may genuinely believe he is acting in the world's best interest, his ability to shape policy without democratic input has raised alarms about the role of private wealth in public life. This tension between philanthropy and democracy is a central theme in debates about Gates's impact.

Bill Gates's influence is vast and multifaceted, reflecting both the power of wealth to drive change and the complexities of balancing public good with personal ambition. His work has undoubtedly improved lives through vaccination campaigns, educational initiatives, and climate innovation. However, his approach has also sparked backlash, highlighting the challenges of relying on private individuals to solve public problems.

Gates's story is a reminder that even well intentioned efforts can have unintended consequences. His impact on public health, education, and climate policy illustrates the power of philanthropy to shape the world, but it also raises important questions about accountability, transparency, and the role of private wealth in public life. As Gates continues to influence global affairs, his legacy will be defined not only by his successes but also by the debates he has ignited about the future of governance and the limits of individual power.

George Soros: The Billionaire Who Redefined Political Influence

George Soros, a Hungarian American financier and philanthropist, has become one of the most influential and polarizing figures in global politics. His journey from surviving the Nazi occupation of Hungary to becoming a hedge fund billionaire and political activist is both fascinating and controversial. Soros's vast fortune has been channeled through his open society foundations, funding progressive movements, media outlets, legal reforms, and social initiatives worldwide. However, his involvement in political activism has sparked fierce backlash, with critics accusing him of using his wealth to push radical agendas and undermine national sovereignty.

Soros was born in 1930 in Budapest, Hungary. As a teenager, he survived the Nazi occupation, a period that shaped his worldview. After fleeing communist Hungary, he studied in London and later made his way to the United States, where he became a financial powerhouse by founding the hedge fund Soros Fund Management. Soros's financial acumen allowed him to accumulate a vast fortune, but it wasn't just his business success that made him famous, it was how he chose to use his wealth.

In 1992, Soros gained international notoriety for his role in "Black Wednesday," when he bet against the British pound and profited by over $1 billion. His aggressive financial strategy forced the United Kingdom to withdraw from the European exchange rate mechanism, leaving a lasting impact on global financial markets. Soros's success cemented his reputation as a master of financial speculation, but it also earned him critics who accused him of destabilizing national economies for profit.

Soros's true influence extends beyond finance. Through his open society foundations, Soros has poured billions of dollars into promoting liberal causes, including human rights, criminal justice reform, immigration advocacy, and media initiatives. His philanthropy has played a major role in shaping political discourse in countries across the globe. Soros supports movements that promote open borders, drug decriminalization, and progressive reforms in law enforcement. His funding of NGOs and activist groups has led to real policy changes, but it has also drawn intense criticism from those who argue that his efforts erode national sovereignty and promote social instability.

In the United States, Soros has become a significant player in local politics by supporting district attorneys who advocate for criminal justice reform. His backing has helped elect prosecutors in cities like San Francisco, Philadelphia, and Los Angeles officials, who emphasize decarceration, the decriminalization of certain offenses, and reduced police involvement. Critics argue that these policies have contributed to rising crime rates and a sense of lawlessness in major cities. Soros's financial involvement in these elections highlights a broader shift in American politics, where wealthy individuals wield enormous influence over local and national policy.

Soros's involvement in global politics has not been without controversy. His advocacy for open borders and refugee resettlement programs has made him a target in Europe, particularly in countries like Hungary and Poland, where nationalist governments view his influence as a threat to their sovereignty. Hungarian Prime Minister Viktor Orbán, in particular, has waged an open campaign against Soros, framing him as a puppet master intent on flooding Europe with migrants to weaken national cultures.

Soros's funding of media outlets and journalism initiatives has also raised concerns about media bias and influence. In some countries, critics argue that Soros funded media organizations have a disproportionate voice in shaping public opinion, often promoting narratives that align with his political beliefs. This dynamic has led to accusations that Soros uses his wealth to manufacture consent for policies that align with his vision of an open society.

George Soros's impact on global politics is undeniable. Through his financial acumen and philanthropic efforts, he has reshaped public policy, challenged national borders, and influenced political movements across the globe. For some, he is a hero who uses his wealth to promote democracy, human rights, and social justice. For others, he is a symbol of unchecked wealth and power, manipulating political systems to serve his ideological interests.

Soros's story exemplifies the complexities of modern influence, where the line between philanthropy and political intervention becomes increasingly blurred. His efforts raise important questions about the role of private wealth in shaping public policy and the consequences of pursuing an ideological vision at the expense of national sovereignty. As Soros's legacy continues to unfold, he remains one of the most controversial figures in the world, a man whose impact will be debated for generations to come.

George Soros's influence goes beyond his role as a billionaire philanthropist, he has profoundly shaped global politics, economics, and public policy through his investments, donations, and political activism.

His Open Society Foundations network spans more than 100 countries, funding initiatives aimed at promoting human rights, democracy, immigration reform, drug decriminalization, and criminal justice reform. However, Soros's activities have not been without significant controversy, with critics accusing him of manipulating political systems and eroding national sovereignty.

In the United States, Soros's involvement in local elections has had a significant impact, particularly in the criminal justice system. He has funneled millions of dollars into the campaigns of progressive district attorneys who advocate for reduced incarceration, cash bail elimination, and alternatives to traditional policing. Soros backed prosecutors like Larry Krasner in Philadelphia, Kim Foxx in Chicago, and George Gascón in Los Angeles, have implemented sweeping reforms that align with Soros's vision of a more lenient justice system.

While these prosecutors argue that their policies are meant to address systemic inequality and racial injustice, critics contend that these reforms have led to rising crime rates and weakened public safety. In cities like San Francisco and Los Angeles, residents have expressed frustration over increased property crime, violent offenses, and a sense of lawlessness. Businesses have even closed stores in areas where theft has become rampant. Soros's impact in this area reveals how political shifts driven by private money can drastically reshape communities.

Soros has also had a significant impact on immigration policy, both in Europe and the United States. Through the open society foundations, he has supported groups that advocate for open borders and refugee resettlement. His funding of pro immigration NGOs has helped shape public discourse, promoting narratives of inclusivity and human rights for migrants and refugees. However, this advocacy has sparked backlash, particularly in Europe, where nationalist movements argue that Soros's policies undermine national sovereignty and cultural identity.

Hungary's Prime Minister Viktor Orbán has become one of Soros's most vocal opponents, accusing him of trying to flood Europe with migrants to weaken traditional values. In 2018, Orbán's government passed the "Stop Soros" law, targeting NGOs that support illegal migration. Soros's advocacy for open borders has made him a symbol of the tension between globalism and nationalism, with his influence seen as both a beacon of humanitarianism and a threat to national autonomy.

Soros's philanthropic reach extends into the media landscape, where he funds independent journalism and advocacy organizations that align with his ideological views. The open society foundations have supported initiatives aimed at promoting transparency, fighting misinformation, and advancing social justice causes. While these efforts have been praised for strengthening civil society, critics argue that Soros's media funding creates bias, giving undue influence to progressive narratives.

This dynamic is particularly evident in contentious political environments, where Soros funded organizations often take positions in favor of progressive policies while marginalizing conservative viewpoints. His involvement in media has drawn scrutiny from those who see his efforts as an attempt to control public opinion and push his vision of an "open society" at the expense of diverse perspectives.

Beyond immigration and media, Soros has invested heavily in democratic reforms in Eastern Europe, Africa, and Latin America. His foundation played a role in the democratization efforts following the collapse of the Soviet Union, funding initiatives that promoted free elections, independent media, and civil liberties. However, Soros's involvement has also fueled accusations of foreign interference. In countries like Russia and Hungary, governments have accused him of undermining their authority by supporting opposition movements and NGOs critical of the regime.

The tension between Soros's philanthropic goals and the backlash from nationalist governments exemplifies the complexities of global philanthropy. While his efforts have advanced democracy in many regions, they have also generated resistance from leaders who view his initiatives as intrusive and politically motivated.

George Soros's impact on the world is profound and multifaceted, reflecting the power of wealth to shape public policy and influence political systems. His philanthropic efforts have undoubtedly advanced human rights, democracy, and social justice. However, they have also sparked significant controversy, raising questions about the role of private individuals in public affairs and the consequences of concentrated influence.

Soros's legacy is a case study in the complexities of modern philanthropy. He has used his fortune not just to address social problems but to reshape political landscapes according to his vision of an open society. This impact underscores both the potential and the dangers of private power in the public sphere. Whether seen as a visionary or a meddling activist, Soros's influence will continue to shape global affairs for years to come.

Margaret Sanger. This chapter would not be complete without talking about Margaret Sanger, a figure whose legacy sits at the intersection of abortion, eugenics, and cultural change. As the founder of what would become Planned Parenthood, Sanger's work in promoting birth control and abortion has made her a hero to some and a deeply controversial figure to others. Her life story, influence, and the ripple effects of her ideas are essential to understanding how the modern conversation around family planning, abortion, and societal values has evolved and how these ideas continue to shape public policy and cultural conflicts today.

Born in 1879, Margaret Sanger grew up in a large, poor family, an experience that deeply shaped her views on family planning. Witnessing her mother's physical deterioration after bearing eleven children, Sanger became convinced that access to birth control was essential for women's health and autonomy. In the early 20th century, discussing contraception was taboo, and distributing information about it was illegal under the Comstock laws, which classified birth control materials as obscene.

Undeterred, Sanger began her campaign for reproductive rights by publishing The Woman Rebel, a radical newsletter advocating for birth control. In 1916, she opened the first birth control clinic in the U.S. in Brooklyn, New York. The clinic was shut down after just nine days, and Sanger was arrested for distributing contraceptive information. However, the publicity around her arrest only fueled her cause. Over the years, Sanger's activism evolved, leading to the establishment of the American Birth Control League in 1921,an organization that would later become Planned Parenthood.

Sanger's legacy is complicated by her association with the eugenics movement, a controversial ideology that sought to improve the genetic quality of the human population. Sanger believed that birth control could help reduce poverty by limiting the reproduction of those she considered unfit to bear children, individuals with mental illness, disabilities, or those living in extreme poverty. Her support for eugenics has drawn intense criticism, with many arguing that her ideas laid the groundwork for systemic discrimination against marginalized communities, particularly people of color and the disabled.

Sanger's defenders argue that she was a product of her time, pointing out that eugenic ideas were widespread in early 20th century intellectual circles. However, her critics maintain that the racist and ableist undertones of her advocacy cannot be ignored. This aspect of her legacy continues to fuel debates about the impact of Planned Parenthood on minority communities, with many pointing to the disproportionate number of abortion clinics in low income and predominantly black neighborhoods.

Planned Parenthood is the largest provider of abortion. The organization credits Sanger with championing women's freedom and bodily autonomy, arguing that access to birth control and abortion is essential to gender equality.

However, the legacy of Sanger's ideas continues to spark controversy. For critics, the promotion of abortion is not a healthcare issue, it's a moral one.

They argue that Sanger's early support for eugenics casts a long shadow over Planned Parenthood's work, raising uncomfortable questions about whether abortion disproportionately affects marginalized communities. Some christian and pro life groups see her as a figure whose ideas have contributed to what they consider a culture of death, where human life, particularly the lives of the unborn and the vulnerable, is treated as disposable.

In the context of this book, Sanger's story serves as a critical example of how cultural ideas, once introduced, can have far reaching and unintended consequences. While her advocacy for birth control sought to empower women, it also opened the door to a broader conversation about population control, family planning, and abortion conversations that have divided the nation ever since. Her story illustrates the power of ideas to shape public policy and cultural norms, for better or worse.

Sanger's legacy is also a stark reminder of the church's absence in shaping certain aspects of cultural morality. While activists like Sanger were promoting radical changes to societal values, much of the church remained silent or disengaged from the conversation, leaving a void that secular ideologies were all too eager to fill. In this way, Sanger's impact highlights the importance of engaging in cultural debates before alternative narratives become dominant.

Her influence is evident today in the ongoing debates over abortion, contraception, and reproductive rights. The divides these debates create reflect deeper philosophical and theological questions about the nature of life, human dignity, and the role of personal freedom. Whether one views Sanger as a hero or a villain, her impact on the cultural landscape is undeniable and understanding her story is essential to grasping the dynamics of today's cultural battles.

Margaret Sanger's legacy is deeply embedded in the modern discourse around abortion, public health, and social justice. However, her impact extends beyond simply advocating for contraception. Sanger's work intertwines with movements like eugenics, leading to a lasting, complex legacy that has shaped how society approaches issues of family planning, abortion, and women's health, while raising difficult questions about ethics, equality, and justice.

Sanger's most enduring impact is the creation of what would later become Planned Parenthood, a network that takes the lives of innocent unborn babies worldwide. Her advocacy for birth control arose from a deeply personal place, witnessing the physical toll that multiple pregnancies took on her mother and other women in poverty. Sanger saw birth control as a means to liberate women, allowing them to control when and if they had children.

Through her clinics, writings, and public speaking, Sanger mainstreamed the concept of contraception, normalizing what had been a taboo topic. She faced legal battles, was arrested, and her clinics were shut down more than once, but her tenacity paved the way for widespread access to contraception. Planned Parenthood now operates over 600 clinics in the U.S., providing birth control, sexual health education, and abortion services.

However, Sanger's impact on family planning is not without controversy, particularly because of her association with the eugenics movement.

Sanger's support for eugenics, the belief in improving the genetic quality of the human population casts a shadow over her legacy. She believed that controlling reproduction could prevent poverty and illness by reducing the number of children born to people she deemed unfit to parent, including those with disabilities, mental illness, and those living in extreme poverty. Although Sanger distanced herself from the more radical elements of eugenics, such as forced sterilizations, her writings reflect a disturbing endorsement of selective breeding.

Sanger's 1921 speech, "The Morality of Birth Control," argued that society should encourage the "fit" to reproduce while limiting reproduction among the "unfit." This ideology, though not uncommon at the time, has been widely condemned for promoting discrimination against marginalized communities, especially people of color and the disabled. Some of her supporters claim that Sanger's involvement with eugenics was a tactical alliance to gain funding and legitimacy for her birth control efforts, but the consequences of this association remain a point of contention.

The eugenics philosophy continues to spark debate about Planned Parenthood's historical and current practices. Critics argue that the organization's focus on reproductive services, including abortion, disproportionately affects minority communities. Although Planned Parenthood emphasizes health equity, many of its clinics are located in low income neighborhoods, raising concerns that the organization perpetuates a system that disproportionately reduces minority populations.

Sanger's work laid the intellectual and cultural foundation for the legalization of abortion in the U.S. Though she personally focused more on contraception than abortion, her advocacy for reproductive freedom set the stage for later movements that sought to legalize abortion as part of women's healthcare. Planned Parenthood became a central figure in this fight, eventually leading to the landmark 1973 Roe v. Wade decision that legalized abortion nationwide.

Even today, the organization's impact is felt in the ongoing debates over abortion rights. The recent overturning of Roe v. Wade in 2022 has placed Planned Parenthood back at the center of the cultural and political battle over reproductive healthcare. Pro life advocates often point to Sanger's eugenics legacy as a reason to oppose Planned Parenthood, arguing that the organization's roots are morally tainted. Meanwhile, pro abortion advocates credit Sanger's vision with empowering women and providing abortions services to millions.

Margaret Sanger's influence extends beyond healthcare into broader societal shifts around gender roles, sexual freedom, and individual autonomy. Her push for contraception was part of a larger movement that promoted sexual liberation, challenging traditional views of marriage and motherhood. For many women, access to birth control symbolized freedom, freedom to pursue education and careers, freedom from the physical toll of frequent pregnancies, and freedom to make choices about their bodies.

However, Sanger's ideas have also sparked criticism from those who argue that the emphasis on reproductive choice has contributed to a culture that devalues motherhood and family. Some pro life advocates contend that the normalization of contraception and abortion has eroded the sanctity of life, leading to a moral decline in society. The debate over Sanger's legacy reflects the larger conflict between secular individualism and faith based values, particularly in how society views life, sexuality, and responsibility.

Sanger's impact is woven into the fabric of modern American society, reflected in the policies and practices of Planned Parenthood, the cultural acceptance of contraception, and the ongoing battle over abortion rights. Her legacy is a mixture of empowerment and controversy, championing reproductive freedom while being tied to a dark history of eugenics.

Sanger's story exemplifies the power of ideas to shape public policy and cultural norms, but it also serves as a cautionary tale about the unintended consequences of those ideas. The tension between freedom and responsibility, between individual rights and collective good, lies at the heart of the debates Sanger's work has ignited.

Her influence will continue to spark debate for generations to come, as society grapples with questions about the value of life, the ethics of abortion, and the role of government and institutions in regulating abortion . Whether viewed as a pioneer of women's rights or a proponent of troubling ideologies, Sanger's impact on the world cannot be denied.

How do you like that? Yeah, we've only scratched the surface here, talking about these people who want to control your life. Take Bill Gates for example, this guy says he's worried about the environment, but that doesn't stop him from flying around in private jets and maintaining multiple mansions. Funny how environmental responsibility works for the rest of us though, huh? And then there's George Soros, a spooky dude if ever there was one, pumping millions into campaigns to reshape our society and push through policies that seem custom designed to erode everything we hold dear.

And let's not forget Elizabeth Bartholet, who's on a mission to end homeschooling. She talks a great game about children needing exposure to diverse viewpoints. But how about this, why don't we waltz into Harvard and host a Bible study? Somehow, I don't think that's quite the diversity she had in mind. Then we've got Hollywood actresses out there, proudly promoting abortion. And don't give me that "pro choice" nonsense! What choice does the baby have?

We've touched on John Dewey, who dragged Marxist ideology into our education system. For anyone who wants to go deeper on that, a good follow up book would be, The Marxification of Education by James Lindsay. And how about Emily Drabinski, the self declared Marxist now running the American Library Association? She's pushing sexually explicit books on kids and championing drag queen story hours. But I'm sure she's not worried about any pushback from the church. .

And then there's Margaret Sanger, the founder of Planned Parenthood. She pushed abortion as a way to "help" low income families. Was she unaware that history is full of people having children with no money? Turns out you don't need a fat bank account to raise a family. But Planned Parenthood is more interested in population control than empowering families.

And what do you say about Randi Weingarten and her political machine masquerading as a teachers' union? She's not just advocating for better working conditions, she's knee deep in left wing activism, and her wife, a lesbian rabbi, only adds another layer of mockery to God's design for marriage.

This is what I want to drive home. These people, the anti God crowd, don't stop! They are relentless. They wake up every day looking for new ways to reshape society, to erode values, to push policies that oppose God's truth. They never take a day off! And where is the church? Nowhere to be found. These activists don't have the power of Almighty God behind them, yet look how much ground they've taken. They press forward without fear. Meanwhile, the very people who have access to the power of the living God sit on the sidelines, silent and irrelevant, watching from the shadows.

Isn't it ironic that those with the ultimate power, God's power, are the ones making the least difference? We say we believe in an all powerful God, but when it comes to confronting evil, we act like we've got nothing to say. If we keep this up, if we remain silent and lukewarm, then Revelation 3:16 tells us exactly what's coming. "Because you are lukewarm, neither hot nor cold, I am about to vomit you out of my mouth." That warning isn't just hypothetical, it's for us. The church is supposed to be a force for truth and righteousness. Instead, we've grown comfortable, passive, and irrelevant.

CHAPTER 9 :

Less Plastic Bags and More Baby Parts

In our modern society, the debate over environmental concerns often takes center stage, with heated discussions about climate change, plastic pollution, and sustainability. While caring for the environment is certainly important, many christians and conservatives have noticed a troubling inconsistency in the moral priorities of those who champion these causes. This chapter explores the paradox in a culture that seems more outraged over the use of plastic bags than the widespread and legalized destruction of unborn children through abortion.

Environmentalism has, in many ways, become the new moral compass for a large segment of society. While caring for the earth is certainly a biblical mandate, Genesis 2:15, environmentalism in the secular world has taken on a religious fervor, often prioritizing the planet over human life itself. In this worldview, reducing plastic waste, cutting carbon emissions, and protecting wildlife have become moral imperatives that trump nearly all other issues.

In contrast, the issue of abortion, the destruction of millions of unborn children each year, receives far less attention from the same voices that decry the dangers of plastic pollution. Many who are quick to campaign for the environment are conspicuously silent when it comes to the issue of abortion, or worse, they actively support it as a fundamental right. This raises a crucial question, how did we get to a point where society is more concerned with environmental causes than the sanctity of human life?

In the book Red Hot Lies, How Global Warming Alarmists Use Threats, Fraud, and Deception to Keep You Misinformed, Christopher Horner exposes how the global warming narrative is often used to manipulate the public into supporting policies that do little to address actual environmental issues. Horner argues that the environmental movement has shifted its focus away from real problems and instead promotes superficial solutions to make people feel like they are contributing to a cleaner planet. For example, Horner points out that the push to ban plastic bags, while touted as a significant environmental victory, has minimal impact compared to the true threats posed by industrial pollution and poor regulatory oversight.

Horner suggests that the obsession with plastic bags and other trivial issues is designed to distract people from more serious concerns. He notes how the media and politicians, by focusing on these feel good measures, allow the public to believe that progress is being made. Meanwhile, the real ethical and societal challenges, such as the industrial scale destruction of human life through abortion, are largely ignored by the same environmental crusaders.

Horner also points to the environmental movement's convenient silence on issues like the exploitation of developing nations for resources. Which directly ties into the selective outrage that accompanies global warming rhetoric. In Red Hot Lies, he reveals how environmental activism is often more about controlling the narrative and pushing specific political agendas than it is about protecting life and ensuring justice.

One of the reasons for this moral inversion is the dehumanization of the unborn child. In the abortion debate, unborn children are often referred to as "clumps of cells" or "tissue," rather than as human beings with inherent dignity and worth. This language is designed to distance people from the reality of what abortion truly is, the taking of an innocent human life.

Just as societies in the past have dehumanized certain groups of people to justify atrocities, e.g., slavery or the Holocaust, today's culture has dehumanized the unborn to justify abortion. In doing so, many people can turn a blind eye to the destruction of life while focusing their attention on less controversial causes, such as environmentalism. The result is a culture that is more concerned with the fate of sea turtles than with the lives of unborn children.

There is an ironic cruelty in the fact that some of the most passionate advocates for environmental protection are often the same people who champion abortion rights. These individuals will go to great lengths to protect endangered species, promote recycling, and ban plastic straws, all while ignoring, or even celebrating, the destruction of unborn human life.

This misplaced compassion reveals a deeper moral confusion. Protecting the environment is important, but it cannot and should not take precedence over protecting human life. The Bible teaches that human beings are made in the image of God, Genesis 1:27, and therefore, every human life is of infinite value. Yet, in the eyes of much of the modern world, an eagle's egg has more legal protection than a human fetus.

It's a tragic sign of our times that the push for environmental sustainability has become a greater rallying cry than the fight for the unborn. Our society has lost its moral compass when it can justify the killing of millions of babies while pouring immense resources into saving endangered animals and reducing plastic waste.

The church must stand as a beacon of truth in a culture that has lost its way. Christians have a biblical mandate to defend the innocent and speak out against injustice, Proverbs 31:8-9. This includes standing up for the most vulnerable among us, the unborn. The church cannot remain silent on the issue of abortion while the world around it focuses on lesser issues.

In addition, the church has a unique opportunity to demonstrate what true compassion looks like. While many environmentalists are driven by fear and guilt, fear of environmental catastrophe and guilt over human impact on the planet, christians are called to a higher form of compassion, one rooted in the love of God and the intrinsic value of every human life.

The church must be clear in its message, while we are called to steward the earth, we are also called to protect human life. The two are not mutually exclusive, but when they are in conflict, the sanctity of life must take precedence. Human beings are the pinnacle of God's creation, and our concern for the environment should never lead us to devalue or destroy human life.

Seth Gruber, a strong advocate for life, says that the church's silence on abortion is one of the greatest moral failures of our time. He argues that if christians truly believed that abortion was the brutal murder of innocent human beings, they would not be able to remain silent. Gruber points out that millions of babies have been killed while much of the church has either looked the other way or justified their inaction with weak excuses like "God is in control." He doesn't mince words when he says that the church's apathy has contributed to the mass slaughter of the most vulnerable among us.

Gruber holds a mirror up to the church, asking how we can claim to follow Jesus, who stood up for the oppressed and gave His life for the least of these, while we remain comfortable in our pews as the bodies of the unborn are discarded like trash. He calls out pastors and leaders for their fear of losing congregants or facing political backlash, reminding them that their duty is to preach the truth, no matter the cost. "Where are the christians willing to sacrifice for the unborn? Where are the pastors with the courage to speak out against the culture of death?" Gruber demands.

He also touches on the fact that some in the church argue that abortion is a "political issue" and therefore not appropriate for the pulpit. But as Gruber passionately explains, abortion is not just a political issue; it is a fundamental moral issue, a matter of life and death. He asks, "If the church won't stand up for the unborn, then who will?" His challenge to christians is clear, stop hiding behind religious platitudes and start acting. For Gruber, the real tragedy is not just that abortion happens, but that the church, with all its moral authority, has stood by and allowed it to continue.

This call to action is not merely about saving lives, it's about the soul of the church. Gruber believes that the church's response to abortion, or lack thereof, will be one of the defining moral markers of our generation. He urges christians to repent for their silence, to speak out boldly, and to become the voice for those who have none. His words resonate deeply with me, as they should with anyone who believes in the sanctity of life. We cannot claim to follow Christ and ignore the cries of the unborn.

The sheer scale of abortion in the modern world is staggering. Since the Roe v. Wade decision in 1973, more than 60 million abortions have been performed in the United States alone. Worldwide, that number is exponentially higher. To put this into perspective, the number of lives lost to abortion far surpasses the death toll of all the world's major genocides combined.

Yet, despite these shocking numbers, abortion is treated as a normal and even celebrated part of modern life. Major corporations, media outlets, and political leaders routinely support and promote abortion as a fundamental right. This normalization of abortion is perhaps one of the greatest moral tragedies of our time, and it is one that the church must continue to oppose with unwavering conviction.

Another troubling aspect of the environmental movement is its ties to population control. Many prominent environmentalists believe that overpopulation is a primary cause of environmental degradation, and therefore reducing the number of people on the planet is necessary for the survival of the earth. This view is not only anti human, but it also feeds into the pro abortion agenda.

Abortion is often framed as a solution to overpopulation, with the argument that fewer people will lead to a healthier planet. This is a dangerous and dehumanizing philosophy that elevates the earth above the value of human life. Christians must reject this worldview and affirm that every human life is precious, regardless of its impact on the environment.

In The Population Bombed! by Pierre Desrochers and Joanna Szurmak, the authors dismantle the overpopulation myth and expose the flawed reasoning behind it. They argue that the fear of overpopulation has been based on a misunderstanding of human potential and progress for decades. Rather than focusing on the false idea that more people mean fewer resources, Desrochers and Szurmak emphasize that human beings are not just consumers of resources but also producers, innovators, and problem solvers. As population increases, so does the capacity for technological innovation, leading to more efficient resource use and new ways to meet humanity's growing needs.

They trace this false narrative back to the early 20th century, when figures like Thomas Malthus and later Paul Ehrlich in his infamous The Population Bomb argued that rapid population growth would lead to mass starvation, environmental collapse, and resource depletion. But history has proven these claims wrong time and again. For instance, in the 1960s and 1970s, Ehrlich's followers believed that agricultural production would fail to keep up with a growing global population, leading to worldwide famine. Instead, advancements in agriculture, such as the Green Revolution, dramatically increased food production, enabling us to feed billions more people than Ehrlich and his followers thought possible.

Desrochers and Szurmak point out that the same pattern of innovation can be seen in virtually every sector where scarcity fears have taken hold.

Whether it's energy, raw materials, or food, human ingenuity has consistently overcome challenges by developing new technologies and more efficient methods. Far from depleting the world's resources human beings have continually found ways to produce more, using less. For example, advances in energy efficiency and renewable energy sources have allowed societies to meet growing energy demands without exhausting resources. The problem isn't too many people, the problem is bad policies and a lack of trust in human potential.

What's more, the book highlights how the overpopulation narrative has been weaponized to justify harmful and even unethical policies, especially in developing countries. Population control measures, often funded and promoted by wealthy nations and international organizations, have led to atrocities such as forced sterilizations and oppressive family planning programs that violate basic human rights. Desrochers and Szurmak argue that these policies are grounded in the misguided belief that fewer people equates to fewer problems, completely ignoring the fact that every human life has inherent value and potential to contribute to society. The focus on population control they argue, is a dehumanizing and shortsighted approach that ultimately harms the very people it claims to help.

This narrative of overpopulation distracts from real, pressing moral issues, such as the widespread destruction of unborn human life. It creates a culture in which human lives, particularly in the womb, are seen as disposable, and societal problems are blamed on too many people rather than on policy failures.

While the world obsesses over reducing plastic bags, it turns a blind eye to the industrial scale destruction of human life through abortion. Desrochers and Szurmak expose this hypocrisy by revealing how the environmental movement has become a distraction, focusing on minor issues while ignoring the larger moral crisis of our time. The overpopulation narrative feeds into this same devaluation of human life, promoting a worldview that sees people as burdens to the planet rather than as the key to solving its problems.

In the end, The Population Bombed! calls for a rethinking of how we view human life, progress, and innovation. It challenges the church and society to reject the overpopulation myth and instead embrace the value of every human life. This is a powerful message for the church today if we truly believe in the sanctity of life, we cannot remain silent on these issues. We must recognize that our failure to address the lies of the overpopulation movement and the horrors of abortion has contributed to the moral decay we see in society today. This call to action, grounded in the truths exposed by Desrochers and Szurmak, aligns with my own plea for the church to wake up and speak out against the culture of death that continues to dominate our world.

It is time for christians, and indeed all people of conscience, to reorder their moral priorities. While caring for the environment is important, it cannot take precedence over the protection of human life. The church must lead the way in affirming the sanctity of life and exposing the moral hypocrisy of a culture that values reducing plastic waste more than the lives of unborn children.

We must also challenge the broader culture to rethink its priorities. The fight against abortion is not just a political issue, it is a moral and spiritual battle for the soul of our nation and the world. If we are to restore a sense of true justice and compassion, we must start by protecting the most vulnerable among us.

The environmental movement has brought some important issues to the forefront, but it has also revealed a deep moral confusion in our society. The church must stand firm in the conviction that human life, especially the life of the unborn, is of greater value than any environmental cause. As we continue to steward the earth, we must do so with a proper understanding of the hierarchy of values, human life comes first.

In the end, it is not just about less plastic or saving the whales, it's about saving the souls of our nation and returning to a culture that values life in all its forms. The church has a critical role to play in this, and the time to act is now. We must speak up for those who cannot speak for themselves and ensure that the sanctity of life is preserved for future generations.

CHAPTER 10 :

Don't Go There, The Rise Of Lawlessness

In many parts of the world, particularly in Western nations, certain areas have come to be known as "no go zones", places where the local authorities have either lost control or are too afraid to enforce the law. These zones, often characterized by high crime rates, violence, or radical ideologies, are becoming increasingly common in cities across Europe and even in parts of the United States. This chapter will explore the rise of these no go zones, the factors contributing to their growth, and the church's role in addressing the moral and societal decay that gives birth to such areas.

No go zones first gained attention in European countries like France, Belgium, and Sweden, where high concentrations of immigrants and refugees from non Western cultures settled in certain neighborhoods. Over time, these areas became isolated from the rest of society, with a growing hostility towards law enforcement and the rule of law. Local authorities, fearing accusations of racism or cultural insensitivity, often turned a blind eye to rising crime, radicalization, and the establishment of parallel societies governed by foreign legal or religious codes.

These zones are not limited to Europe, however. In the United States, cities like Chicago, Detroit, and Baltimore have experienced similar trends in certain neighborhoods. High levels of crime, gang activity, and distrust of the police have created areas where local residents fear to tread, and where law enforcement is either stretched too thin or unwilling to engage.

As these zones expand, they become breeding grounds for further lawlessness and radicalization, where extremism, organized crime, and moral decay take root, unchecked by any governing authority. The church, as a moral and spiritual authority, must recognize the severity of this issue and rise to meet the challenge.

At the heart of the no go zone phenomenon is a deeper spiritual and moral issue, lawlessness. The Bible speaks clearly about the consequences of lawlessness and the importance of order, justice, and righteousness in society, Matthew 24:12, Romans 13:1-7. When a community rejects these values, chaos and disorder soon follow. No go zones are the natural outcome of a society that has turned away from its moral foundations.

In many of these areas, we see not just the absence of law enforcement, but the absence of moral order. Drug trafficking, prostitution, violence, and other forms of criminal activity flourish in environments where the rule of law is undermined. The failure of local governments and law enforcement to assert control over these areas is often a symptom of a larger cultural problem. The rejection of traditional moral values, particularly those rooted in a biblical worldview.

This moral decay is often exacerbated by political correctness, which prevents authorities from confronting the root causes of these problems. Rather than addressing the breakdown of the family, the rise of radical ideologies, or the glorification of violence in popular culture, politicians and media figures often downplay the seriousness of the issue or shift the blame elsewhere.

The church cannot afford to ignore the rise of no go zones or retreat in fear from these troubled areas. As followers of Christ, we are called to go into the darkest places of society and bring the light of the gospel, Matthew 5:14-16. The church must be willing to engage with these communities, not just spiritually, but also practically, by offering support, guidance, and a moral compass that can lead people out of lawlessness and into a life of peace and order.

The first step for the church is to address the spiritual needs of these areas. Prayer, evangelism, and discipleship are essential components of any effort to reclaim no go zones. Churches must be willing to plant themselves in the heart of these troubled communities, offering hope and the message of salvation to those who are trapped in cycles of violence and despair. Only the transforming power of the gospel can change the hearts of individuals and by extension, the communities in which they live.

Alongside spiritual engagement, the church must also offer practical support to these communities. This can include programs that address poverty, addiction, family breakdown, and education. Many of the people living in no go zones are trapped by economic and social conditions that leave them feeling powerless and disenfranchised. The church can offer a way out by providing resources, mentorship, and opportunities for personal and community growth.

The church can also play a role in bridging the gap between law enforcement and the local community. In many no go zones there is deep distrust between residents and the police, which only worsens the situation. Churches can serve as mediators, working with both sides to restore trust, promote dialogue, and encourage a cooperative approach to solving problems. By working together with local authorities, churches can help restore law and order in these areas, while also addressing the underlying spiritual and moral issues.

Finally, the church must not be afraid to speak out against the cultural and political forces that contribute to the rise of no go zones. Whether it's the glorification of violence in media, the breakdown of the family, or the failure of local governments to enforce the law, the church must be a prophetic voice, calling society back to its moral foundations. This will require courage and conviction, as many of these issues are deeply entrenched in the political and cultural landscape.

If the church remains silent or inactive, the consequences will be dire. No go zones will continue to expand, and the lawlessness that characterizes them will spread to other parts of society. The breakdown of moral order in these areas is not an isolated phenomenon, it is a warning of what can happen when a society turns its back on God and His principles.

Throughout history, societies that have embraced lawlessness and moral decay have eventually collapsed. The Bible warns that sin, when left unchecked, leads to destruction, Romans 6:23. If the church does not take a stand now, we risk seeing entire cities, and perhaps even nations, fall into chaos.

But the church has the power to make a difference. Throughout history, the church has been at the forefront of movements for social change, justice, and revival. From the early christian church that stood against the Roman Empire's brutality, to the abolitionist movements that fought against slavery, to the civil rights movements of the 20th century, christians have consistently been the ones to step into the darkest places of society and shine the light of truth.

While the rise of no go zones may seem like a sign of societal decline, there is hope. God has not abandoned these communities, and neither should the church. The Bible teaches that where sin abounds, grace abounds even more, Romans 5:20. This means that even in the most troubled areas, God's power to redeem and restore is greater than the forces of evil that seek to destroy.

The church must approach this challenge with faith, courage, and a renewed sense of mission. By engaging with no go zones, both spiritually and practically, the church can help bring about transformation in these communities. It won't be easy, and the path forward may be fraught with obstacles, but the church has a unique role to play in reclaiming these areas for Christ.

The rise of no go zones is a symptom of a larger spiritual and moral crisis in our society. But it is also an opportunity for the church to step into the breach and bring the healing power of the gospel to these troubled areas. By engaging with these communities, partnering with local authorities, and standing up for truth, the church can help turn the tide and restore peace and order where lawlessness once reigned.

It is time for the church to stop retreating from these challenges and to start advancing with boldness and faith. If we do, we will see not just the transformation of no go zones, but the renewal of entire cities and nations. The battle is not just against flesh and blood, but against spiritual forces of darkness, Ephesians 6:12. The church, empowered by the Holy Spirit, is uniquely equipped to win this battle.

CHAPTER 11 :

People Who Make A Difference

Allow me to take the Liberty here, and kick off this chapter with a part of a talk I did on my video, Symposium On The Sea episode 4.

I thank God for people whose words have inspired me. I thank God for my dad, he was an example of a faithful husband, father, and who was faithful to his God. I'm grateful to the many Bible teachers on the radio who have ministered to me. I'm grateful to people like Glenn Beck, Steve Deace, and others, who boldly call out evil and encourage faith in God. I'm grateful for authors of books, like Thomas Sowell, Liz Wheeler, and others too many dimension.

These people say uncomfortable things, stick their neck out, and have a backbone. They inform the uninformed, and inspire people, and are greatly needed in our world today.

I have a pet peeve about those people who are seemingly always happy, seems a bit artificial in light of all that's going on in our world today. They're exuberant about every little thing God did for them that morning, including finding them a place to park. You know, the people who seem to have a faith a mile wide and an inch deep.

When I talk to these people about our country, and how the church should speak up about it, it just doesn't register with them. They're just happy, happy, happy. I usually get a big smile, and they say things like, God is in control.

Yeah, why get up tight about it right?

These same people usually think that before any disaster comes to this country or to where they live, they will be raptured away. Sure that'd be nice huh?

Somehow I don't think it's going to go down like that. I believe the crowd with a smile saying God is in control is the problem.

God is a control is just an excuse christians give in the free world to justify sitting on their butt while the country goes to hell in a handbasket.

In an age where cultural decay and moral compromise seem to be the norm, there are still individuals and groups who refuse to be silenced. These people have chosen to stand in the gap, boldly defending truth and justice in a world that often seeks to silence dissent. This chapter highlights the stories of modern day heroes, ordinary people who have made extraordinary contributions in the fight against evil, immorality, and tyranny. Their examples serve as a call to action for the church and its members to join the battle for righteousness in today's world.

Moms for Liberty: Defending Parental Rights

Moms for Liberty is a grassroots organization that has gained national attention for its fight to protect parental rights in education. Founded by concerned mothers, the group focuses on pushing back against the increasingly radical and inappropriate material being taught in public schools, including the sexualization of children and the introduction of critical race theory.

By organizing local chapters, attending school board meetings, and advocating for transparency in curriculum, Moms for Liberty has been instrumental in holding school officials accountable. These mothers have refused to let their children be indoctrinated by harmful ideologies, and their efforts have inspired other parents across the nation to take a stand as well.

Their success is a testament to the power of community action, and the impact that a small dedicated group of people can have when they unite around a common cause. Moms for Liberty has proven that even ordinary citizens when informed and organized, can make a significant difference in protecting the next generation.

A notable story involving Moms for Liberty took place in Brevard county Florida, where the organization successfully advocated for the removal of controversial books from school libraries.

In 2021, Moms for Liberty chapters in Florida raised concerns about books that contained explicit sexual content, violent themes, and ideologically biased narratives being made available to young students in public school libraries. The group argued that many of these books were inappropriate for children, particularly in elementary and middle schools, and that parents had the right to know what materials were accessible to their kids. They also questioned the lack of transparency in the school district's selection process for these books.

One book that came under scrutiny was "Gender Queer," a graphic novel that the group argued contained sexually explicit content inappropriate for school aged children. Moms for Liberty members attended school board meetings, submitted formal complaints, and shared excerpts from the books in question to highlight the graphic nature of the material. Their efforts garnered attention from both local media and parents, sparking a heated debate about censorship, educational materials, and parental rights.

Through persistence, and despite opposition, Moms for Liberty was able to convince the Brevard County school district to review and remove certain books from the library shelves that were inappropriate for minors. The district also established a formal process for parents to challenge books they found concerning and implemented stricter guidelines for reviewing future materials.

This victory was seen as a triumph for parental involvement in education, as it gave parents a greater voice in the content their children were exposed to at school. The story also highlighted a larger cultural battle over who gets to decide what is appropriate for children in public education, parents or the state.

Cornerstone Chapel and Pastor Gary Hamrick: A Church Making a Difference

Gary Hamrick and Cornerstone Chapel in Leesburg Virginia, exemplify the growing movement of churches that refuse to remain silent on political and cultural issues. In a time when many churches shy away from discussing politics from the pulpit, Hamrick boldly speaks out on topics such as abortion, gender ideology, marriage, religious freedom, and the importance of civic engagement. For Hamrick and his congregation, these matters are not just political, they are deeply spiritual and moral issues that demand the church's attention.

Hamrick's messages emphasize that the church has a responsibility to be a moral compass for society. He argues that christians cannot compartmentalize their faith and leave it outside the political realm, especially when public policies directly contradict biblical teachings. Cornerstone Chapel has become known for encouraging its members to be informed voters and actively participate in shaping the future of the nation by engaging with key social issues. Hamrick frequently stresses that the deterioration of society is connected to the church's reluctance to stand up for biblical truth.

During the COVID-19 pandemic, Hamrick's leadership was put to the test when Virginia imposed restrictions on church gatherings. While many churches complied with prolonged shutdowns, Cornerstone Chapel reopened its doors relatively early, emphasizing the essential nature of worship and the church's role in community support. This decision drew both praise and criticism, but for Hamrick, it was a matter of prioritizing faith over fear. He expressed that the government's inconsistency, keeping liquor stores open while deeming churches non essential highlighted the need for christians to take a stand.

Hamrick has also used his platform to address the importance of defending life, often speaking passionately about the sanctity of the unborn. Cornerstone Chapel partners with local pro life organizations, providing resources and support to pregnant women in crisis and advocating for the overturning of pro abortion legislation. These efforts are part of the church's broader commitment to being a positive force in the community by offering real world solutions that align with biblical values.

In his sermons, Hamrick is not afraid to confront controversial topics head on. He frequently discusses the church's responsibility to oppose cultural trends that contradict Scripture, such as the normalization of gender fluidity and the redefinition of marriage. He argues that these issues are not just political matters but spiritual battles that require the church's active participation. Hamrick draws parallels between today's challenges and historical moments when the church played a crucial role in resisting tyranny and injustice, such as the church's role in the abolitionist movement and the civil rights era.

Hamrick's leadership has also extended beyond the walls of Cornerstone Chapel. He encourages christians to run for public office and engage in local government, believing that change begins at the grassroots level. His church regularly hosts events and voter drives aimed at educating believers about their civic responsibilities and the importance of voting according to biblical principles. Hamrick's influence has been felt not only within his church but also in the broader evangelical community, where his unapologetic stance has inspired other pastors to engage more actively in political discourse.

Cornerstone Chapel's community outreach efforts reflect its commitment to being a church that makes a tangible difference. From supporting local food banks and shelters to partnering with crisis pregnancy centers, the church seeks to live out its faith in practical ways. Hamrick often reminds his congregation that being "salt and light" requires action, not just words.

Through Hamrick's leadership, Cornerstone Chapel demonstrates that churches can be both spiritually vibrant and socially engaged, making a difference not only within their congregations but also in the broader community. Their impact serves as a reminder that the church, when it chooses to engage, has the power to shape culture, influence policy, and bring about real change.

Calvary Chapel Chino Hills and Jack Hibbs: A Church on the Frontlines of Cultural Engagement

Jack Hibbs, the senior pastor of Calvary Chapel Chino Hills in California, has become a leading voice among evangelical Christians who believe the church must take an active role in addressing cultural and political issues. His story is one of boldness, conviction, and a willingness to challenge the status quo, even when that stance provokes controversy. For Hibbs, the call to preach the gospel goes hand in hand with speaking out on moral and social issues, from the sanctity of life to religious freedom, gender, and marriage. His unapologetic engagement with these topics has made him both a hero to many christians and a target of criticism from secular and progressive circles.

Hibbs frequently argues that the decline of American culture is directly linked to the silence of the church. At Calvary Chapel Chino Hills, political engagement is woven into the fabric of ministry. From the pulpit, Hibbs tackles hot button issues that other pastors might avoid, such as abortion, LGBTQ activism, and California's progressive policies. Hibbs believes that these are not merely political issues but deeply spiritual matters that the Bible addresses directly. He is known to challenge his congregation to vote according to biblical principles. And to hold elected officials accountable for laws that oppose God's design for life, family, and governance.

The COVID-19 pandemic became a defining moment for Hibbs and his church. In defiance of California's strict lockdown mandates, which limited church gatherings while allowing businesses like liquor stores and marijuana dispensaries to remain open, Calvary Chapel Chino Hills reopened its doors early. Hibbs argued that the state's decision to deem churches "non essential" was both unconstitutional and a direct attack on religious freedom.

He framed the decision to keep his church open not as an act of rebellion but as an essential act of obedience to God. The church became a gathering place for thousands of people seeking spiritual refuge during a time of fear and uncertainty. Though Hibbs faced criticism and legal threats, he remained firm, saying, "The church is not only essential, it is transcendent." His decision garnered national attention and support from other pastors, reinforcing the idea that the church must resist when the government oversteps its bounds.

One of Hibbs's primary concerns is the sanctity of life. He is a passionate advocate for the pro life movement, regularly using his platform to speak out against abortion. He often partners with organizations working to end abortion and support mothers in crisis, emphasizing the need for the church to be both outspoken and compassionate. Hibbs's approach to activism is holistic, encouraging believers to engage not just in public protests or voting but in practical ways, such as volunteering at pregnancy resource centers and supporting foster care initiatives.

In addition to life issues, Hibbs has taken a firm stand on family and gender. He speaks frequently about the biblical model of marriage and the dangers of gender ideology, warning that the normalization of these issues erodes the foundation of society. His sermons often include calls for parents to become actively involved in their children's education, advocating for parental rights and transparency in public schools.

Hibbs believes that part of the church's mission is to equip believers to engage with the political realm. He regularly hosts voter education events at Calvary Chapel Chino Hills, helping congregants understand the importance of voting according to their faith. The church has become a hub for civic engagement, offering resources and seminars on how to contact legislators, run for office, and influence public policy. Hibbs encourages christians to see their involvement in politics not as an optional activity but as a calling to be "salt and light" in the public square.

In his view, the church must reject the false dichotomy between faith and politics. "We don't have the luxury of staying silent," he often says, arguing that every issue, from marriage to the economy, has spiritual implications. Hibbs's sermons are filled with historical references to the church's role in social movements, from the abolition of slavery to the civil rights era, challenging his congregation to continue that legacy in today's cultural battles.

Hibbs's bold stance on political and cultural issues has not come without opposition. He has been labeled a "christian nationalist" by critics who accuse him of blurring the line between church and state. However, Hibbs rejects this label, insisting that his activism is rooted in biblical truth rather than political ideology. "I don't accept intimidation or labels," he says. "God established the government, and when it turns away from Him, it's the church's responsibility to speak truth."

Despite the criticism, Calvary Chapel Chino Hills continues to grow, attracting believers who are drawn to its clear message and unapologetic engagement with the world. The church has become a beacon for christians who feel called to resist cultural trends that they believe conflict with their faith.

The influence of Jack Hibbs and Calvary Chapel Chino Hills extends far beyond Sunday services. Through online platforms, Hibbs's sermons reach millions of viewers, amplifying his message to a national and international audience. He frequently collaborates with other pastors, political leaders, and advocacy organizations, creating a network of christians committed to cultural renewal. Hibbs's leadership has inspired many believers to become more vocal and active in their communities, encouraging a movement of politically engaged christians.

 For Hibbs, the church is not just a place of worship, it's a launchpad for transformation, equipping believers to be agents of change in a world that desperately needs truth.

First Baptist Dallas and Robert Jeffress: A Church Unafraid to Speak Boldly

Robert Jeffress, the senior pastor of First Baptist Church in Dallas Texas, is one of the most outspoken voices in American evangelicalism. Known for his unapologetic sermons, media appearances, and political endorsements, Jeffress has built a reputation for blending faith with civic responsibility. Under his leadership, First Baptist Dallas has become a powerful platform for promoting conservative values, urging believers to take a stand in politics and culture, and calling out moral decay in society.

Jeffress has long argued that the church cannot be silent on political matters, particularly when they intersect with biblical principles. In his view, moral issues like abortion, marriage, and religious liberty are not just political, they are spiritual battles. His sermons frequently address these topics, warning congregants about the dangers of secularism and the erosion of christian values in America. Jeffress has emphasized that christians have a responsibility to vote for leaders who align with biblical teachings, famously saying, "If you're not at the table, you're on the menu."

His stance has not been without controversy. Jeffress has been criticized for blurring the line between church and state, with some accusing him of promoting christian nationalism. However, Jeffress argues that it is not only permissible but necessary for christians to engage in the political process to ensure that godly principles shape public policy. He often cites historical examples, reminding his audience that the church played a pivotal role in social movements like the abolition of slavery and the civil rights era.

Jeffress's impact reached new heights during the Trump presidency, when he became one of the most vocal evangelical supporters of Donald Trump. He defended Trump's policies as aligned with christian values, especially in areas such as religious freedom, support for Israel, and the appointment of conservative judges. Jeffress frequently appeared in media interviews, speaking on behalf of evangelicals and explaining why many christians supported Trump despite his personal flaws.

During this time, First Baptist Dallas hosted several events that blended faith and patriotism, including a July 4th service celebrating America's christian heritage. These events highlighted Jeffress's belief that the United States has a divine purpose and that christians must fight to preserve that purpose. Critics viewed these services as overly nationalistic, but Jeffress saw them as a call to action for believers to reclaim the moral foundations of the nation.

Religious freedom has been one of the defining issues of Jeffress's ministry. He frequently warns that the secular left is working to erode religious liberties, using policies on gender, sexuality, and public education to marginalize christians. First Baptist Dallas has become a hub for advocacy on these issues, hosting conferences and events to equip believers to defend their faith in the public square.

Jeffress's sermons often focus on the importance of courage in the face of cultural opposition. He draws on biblical examples of individuals who stood up to godless rulers, such as Daniel in Babylon, and challenges his congregation to be fearless in their faith. His messages are designed to inspire christians to engage in the political process, not out of partisanship but out of a desire to see God's truth reflected in law and policy.

Under Jeffress's leadership, First Baptist Dallas has not only grown in size but also in influence. The church offers a wide range of ministries, from support groups for those struggling with addiction to programs that help women facing unplanned pregnancies. These outreach efforts reflect the church's commitment to living out the gospel in practical ways, even as it engages in larger cultural battles.

Through his television and radio programs, Jeffress reaches millions of listeners across the country, amplifying his message beyond the walls of his church. His books and public appearances have also cemented his role as a prominent voice in American evangelicalism. While his bold approach has earned him both admirers and critics, there is no doubt that Robert Jeffress and First Baptist Dallas have had a significant impact on the conversation around faith and politics in America.

Robert Jeffress and First Baptist Dallas offer a powerful example of a church that refuses to retreat from the cultural and political battlefield. Jeffress's leadership demonstrates the influence that faith communities can have when they choose to engage rather than withdraw. His story underscores the theme that silence is not an option for the church in a time of moral and spiritual crisis.

Jeffress believes that the church must be the conscience of the nation, calling it back to God's truth and standing firm against secularism. His unapologetic approach may be controversial, but it exemplifies the kind of bold faith that can inspire believers to make a difference in their communities and the nation at large. Through First Baptist Dallas, Jeffress has built a legacy that reflects both the challenges and the rewards of speaking truth in a culture that often prefers silence.

Harvest Christian Fellowship and Greg Laurie: Balancing Evangelism and Public Engagement

Greg Laurie, pastor of Harvest Christian Fellowship in Riverside California, is known for his passion for evangelism and reaching the lost through large scale crusades and media outreach. While his ministry focuses heavily on spreading the message of salvation through Christ, Laurie has also become a voice in the cultural and political arena, encouraging christians to engage with social issues that intersect with their faith. His journey reflects a balance between the great commission and the call for believers to stand for truth in a society that is increasingly hostile to christian values.

Laurie's ministry began in the 1970s, born out of the Jesus Movement, a revival among young people in Southern California. Over the years, Laurie expanded his ministry through Harvest Crusades, large evangelistic events that have drawn millions of attendees. These events, held in stadiums across the United States, focus on preaching the gospel and inviting people to commit their lives to Christ. Laurie's down to earth preaching style and relatable storytelling have made him a beloved figure among christians and seekers alike.

While evangelism remains the core of Laurie's ministry, he has also recognized that the gospel cannot be separated from the realities of the world. He often speaks on cultural issues, encouraging believers to live out their faith boldly and influence their communities for Christ.

Laurie has addressed several contentious issues from the pulpit and through his media platforms, including marriage, the sanctity of life, and religious freedom. While his approach is less overtly political than some other evangelical leaders, Laurie emphasizes that christians must be involved in shaping culture. He argues that staying silent on important social matters is not right.

Laurie has also publicly defended the biblical definition of marriage and spoken against the normalization of behaviors that contradict scripture. His messages often include reminders that while christians are called to love others, they must also stand firm on biblical truth, even when it is unpopular. Laurie encourages believers to engage in public life not out of partisanship, but out of obedience to God's commands to defend life, honor marriage, and promote justice.

Unlike some pastors who adopt a more confrontational stance, Laurie's engagement with politics is marked by a tone of grace and humility. For example, during the COVID-19 pandemic, Laurie navigated the challenges of church shutdowns and restrictions with careful discernment. While some churches defied state mandates, Harvest Christian Fellowship initially complied with public health guidelines, focusing on online services and outdoor gatherings. Laurie made it clear that the church's mission was to reach people with the gospel, regardless of the circumstances.

However, Laurie also spoke out against policies that he believed unfairly targeted churches or restricted religious freedoms. His balanced approach, complying with regulations where possible but speaking out when necessary, earned respect from both his congregation and the broader christian community.

Laurie's influence extends beyond his local church through his radio program, books, and online content, which reach millions worldwide. His ability to navigate complex cultural issues while keeping the focus on the gospel has made him a trusted voice among christians seeking guidance on how to live faithfully in a challenging world.

Laurie has also been deeply committed to equipping the next generation of believers to engage with culture and share their faith. His ministry regularly hosts conferences, youth events, and training programs designed to prepare young people for leadership. Laurie's heart for the younger generation reflects his belief that the future of the church depends on equipping believers to navigate a world that is increasingly opposed to christian values.

In recent years, Laurie has been candid about the cultural challenges facing young christians, such as the pressure to conform to secular ideologies and the erosion of religious freedom. He encourages young believers to find their identity in Christ and be unafraid to stand for truth, even when it comes at a cost.

Greg Laurie's ministry exemplifies the delicate balance between evangelism and cultural engagement. Through Harvest Christian Fellowship and his national platform, Laurie demonstrates that it is possible to faithfully proclaim the gospel while addressing social and moral issues with grace. His leadership during difficult cultural moments, such as the COVID-19 pandemic and the ongoing debates about religious freedom, shows that the church can adapt to changing circumstances without compromising its mission.

Laurie's story offers a powerful example of how the church can make a difference by staying true to its calling while engaging with the world. His approach encourages believers to focus on the transformative power of the gospel while also standing firm on biblical truth in the public square. For Laurie, the ultimate goal is not political victory, but the salvation of souls and the advancement of God's kingdom, a mission that remains as relevant today as ever.

Donald J. Trump: A Defining Force in the Pro-Life Movement

Donald J. Trump's presidency redefined the political landscape on the issue of abortion, making him one of the most influential figures in the pro life movement. While Trump's early career and personal life didn't suggest a strong ideological commitment to the cause, his actions in office transformed him into a champion for those advocating for the sanctity of life. His legacy in this regard is a crucial part of understanding how political leadership can impact moral and cultural debates in America.

Before entering politics, Trump was not known for being a staunch opponent of abortion. In fact, in a 1999 interview, he described himself as "pro abortion" while acknowledging that his views might evolve. Over time, and particularly during his run for the presidency in 2016, Trump's stance on abortion shifted significantly. By the time he entered the White House, he had embraced the pro life position, arguing that the protection of the unborn was a moral imperative and aligning himself with evangelical voters and other pro life advocates.

Some observers suggest that Trump's evolution on the issue was politically motivated, an effort to galvanize the support of a key conservative voting bloc. However, his actions during his presidency demonstrated a level of commitment that went beyond mere rhetoric. Trump's policies and judicial appointments reflected a deliberate strategy to reshape abortion policy in America.

One of Trump's most significant contributions to the pro life movement was his reshaping of the federal judiciary, particularly the U.S. Supreme Court. Trump nominated three conservative justices, Neil Gorsuch, Brett Kavanaugh, and Amy Coney Barrett. Their confirmations shifted the ideological balance of the Court, creating a majority more sympathetic to pro life arguments.

The culmination of these efforts came in 2022, when the Supreme Court overturned Roe v. Wade in the Dobbs v. Jackson Women's Health Organization decision. Although the ruling occurred after Trump left office, the groundwork was laid by the justices he appointed. The Dobbs decision returned the authority to regulate abortion to individual states, effectively dismantling the federal protection for abortion that had been in place since 1973. For many in the pro life movement, this was the victory they had been seeking for nearly five decades.

During his time in office, Trump also took steps to limit federal funding for organizations that provide abortions, particularly Planned Parenthood. His administration reinstated and expanded the "Mexico City Policy," which prohibits U.S. funding of foreign NGOs that perform or promote abortion. Domestically, his administration sought to block Title X funding from clinics that offer abortion services, further restricting the resources available to organizations like Planned Parenthood.

Trump's administration also supported legislation aimed at protecting the unborn, including bills that would ban late term abortions. He was the first sitting president to speak in person at the annual March for Life in Washington D.C., where he declared "Every life is worth protecting." His appearance marked a historic moment as previous presidents even those who supported the pro life movement, had typically avoided direct involvement in the event.

Trump's stance on abortion and his actions in office deepened the divide between pro life and pro abortion advocates. Supporters viewed him as a fearless champion for life, willing to take bold steps where other leaders had faltered. His administration gave new momentum to the pro life movement, inspiring state legislatures to pass stricter abortion laws and emboldening activists who had long felt marginalized.

However, Trump's outspoken approach also intensified opposition from pro abortion advocates, who saw his policies as an attack on women's rights. The battle over abortion became one of the defining cultural conflicts of his presidency, and the Dobbs decision, enabled by Trump's judicial appointments, remains one of the most contentious legal developments in recent history.

Trump's pro life record endeared him to many evangelical leaders, including those who had previously been skeptical of his personal character. Pastors like Robert Jeffress and Jack Hibbs praised Trump's efforts, urging their congregations to support him as a leader who aligned with biblical values. For many pro life christians, Trump's presidency was a testament to the importance of electing leaders willing to stand for truth, even in the face of opposition.

At the same time, Trump's polarizing style alienated other christian leaders, who argued that his personal behavior and divisive rhetoric undermined the moral authority of his policies. The debate over Trump's legacy within the church reflects a broader tension about the role of political power in advancing moral objectives.

Donald J. Trump's impact on the pro life movement is undeniable. Through his judicial appointments, policy changes, and public advocacy, Trump shifted the national conversation on abortion and paved the way for historic legal changes. His legacy serves as a reminder that leadership matters, one individual in a position of power can shape the moral and cultural landscape of a nation.

Trump's story is a powerful example of how political engagement can yield tangible results in the fight against moral decline. Whether one agrees with all of Trump's policies or not, his actions demonstrate that silence is not an option when it comes to issues of life and justice. For the pro life movement, Trump's presidency was not just a political victory, it was a watershed moment that redefined the future of the movement and challenged the church to engage more deeply in the cultural battles of the day.

Elon Musk. When it comes to Elon Musk, I can't help but admire the man for his brilliance and innovative spirit. Here's a guy who's used his mind not just to create businesses but to push boundaries, change industries, and open doors most of us didn't even know existed. Whether it's Tesla, SpaceX, or Starlink, Musk has demonstrated that thinking outside the box can lead to extraordinary things. He's taken risks and reimagined the future in ways few would dare, and that's something worth respecting.

Now, I get that Musk is concerned about the environment, and I can appreciate that. But personally, I don't buy into the whole narrative of man made climate change. I believe it's being used as a tool to control people and push unnecessary regulations. The way climate alarmism is being weaponized feels more like a power grab than genuine environmental concern. That said, I respect Musk's approach. He isn't just preaching about environmental issues, he's innovating, offering practical solutions through electric cars and battery technology. He's someone who's actually doing something, not just demanding that governments slap on new restrictions to solve the world's problems.

I also understand that Musk leaned more to the left in his earlier days. But what I admire most about him now is how his views have shifted more towards conservatism and freedom. He's grown increasingly skeptical of government overreach and cancel culture, and it's refreshing to see someone with his influence embrace the importance of free speech. That's what makes Musk stand out, he's not afraid of opposing ideas. His philosophy seems to be, put all the ideas on the table, and let the best one win. That's a mindset we desperately need more of today, especially in an environment where people are silenced for saying things that go against the narrative.

Look at what he's done with Starlink. It's not just some high tech satellite project, it's changing the way people communicate, especially in places where traditional internet infrastructure is unavailable or controlled. It's been used in war torn regions, during natural disasters, and in rural areas to keep people connected. That kind of tool makes a real difference in people's lives, providing communication and freedom in ways that most of us take for granted.

And let's not forget how he's aligning more and more with conservative principles. His support for freedom of speech and his willingness to stand against the tide of censorship puts him in the same camp as leaders like Donald Trump. I don't just admire Musk's brain, I admire his willingness to put his influence behind what he believes is right, even when it's unpopular. I genuinely believe Musk wants what's best for this country. He seems to understand that without freedom,freedom of thought, speech, and innovation,there is no progress. Musk's vision isn't just about making money, it's about creating a future where ideas flourish, where people are free to think, argue, and create without fear of being silenced. And in a time when so many voices are being shut down, that kind of leadership matters.

Patriot Mobile: Putting Money Where Your Values Are

Patriot Mobile is a wireless company with a mission to defend conservative values and support organizations that fight for religious liberty, freedom of speech, and the sanctity of life. Unlike other major corporations that often funnel money toward causes and ideologies that undermine traditional values, Patriot Mobile is committed to supporting christian organizations, pro life initiatives, and groups that stand for freedom.

Through their "Patriot Mobile Gives Back" program, a portion of every customer's bill goes directly to support causes like the NRA, the Susan B. Anthony List, and organizations that fight for religious freedom in court. The company's model proves that capitalism can be a force for good when it is aligned with moral and biblical principles.

Patriot Mobile encourages consumers to think about how their spending habits can impact the culture. By choosing to support companies and organizations that reflect christian values, individuals can contribute to the broader fight against moral and cultural decline. Patriot Mobile is a reminder that christians can make a difference, not just through activism, but through the choices they make every day in the marketplace.

One significant battle Patriot Mobile has fought occurred in Texas, where the company aligned itself with conservative values by supporting local school board races to counter progressive ideologies infiltrating public schools.

In 2022, Patriot Mobile became involved in the Tarrant County school board elections, where several seats were up for grabs. This wasn't just a local election, it was a microcosm of the national battle over education, values, and parental rights. Patriot Mobile, as part of its mission to support christian conservative values, recognized that public schools were becoming ideological battlegrounds. The curriculum was increasingly infused with topics like critical race theory, gender ideology, and political activism, which many conservative parents opposed.

To combat what they saw as a progressive agenda in schools, Patriot Mobile launched a political action committee PAC called Patriot Mobile Action. The PAC's goal was to support conservative candidates for school boards, ensuring that these local leaders would stand for traditional American values, parental rights, and transparent education. In Tarrant County, a diverse area of Texas that includes Fort Worth and its suburbs, Patriot Mobile Action funded and supported a slate of conservative candidates who ran on platforms that promised to challenge progressive curriculum choices, protect parental involvement, and keep politically charged content out of the classroom.

Patriot Mobile Action contributed financial resources, grassroots campaigning, and community organizing to mobilize conservative voters. Their support was crucial in an election that became a battleground between progressive and conservative visions of what public education should look like. On the progressive side, there was a push for diversity, equity, and inclusion programs, as well as a curriculum that emphasized systemic racism and LGBTQ issues. On the conservative side, candidates backed by Patriot Mobile ran on preserving what they saw as core American values, fighting against CRT, and giving parents more control over what their children were being taught.

Patriot Mobile Action's involvement paid off. In a series of closely watched races, the conservative candidates won, flipping control of the school board to a more traditional, pro parental rights majority. The victory was a significant moment in the broader culture war, symbolizing the power of grassroots activism and local involvement in education.

What made this battle particularly important was that it wasn't just about one school district, it sent a message across Texas and the nation that parents and local communities can fight back against what they perceive as ideological overreach in schools. The win emboldened other conservative activists and organizations to replicate the model Patriot Mobile had used, focusing on local elections, backing conservative candidates, and mobilizing voters to effect change from the ground up.

I talked about Patriot Mobile in my church one time. I explained how it was one of the few phone companies that actively supports christian values, donating to pro life causes, conservative candidates, and fighting for religious freedoms. In contrast, I pointed out that major telecom companies like AT&T, Verizon, and T Mobile have been known to contribute to organizations that support abortion, LGBTQ activism, and other progressive agendas that directly conflict with biblical teachings. I expected some shock, or at the very least, interest from the people I spoke to. But instead, what I got was indifference.

The church members I talked to, seem to shrug it off. "It's just a phone company," one person said. "It's not my problem how they spend their money. I just want my phone to work." It was as if they couldn't, or wouldn't, see the connection between their spending and the growing influence of these progressive agendas. They failed to recognize that by continuing to use these companies, they were funding the very things that christians should stand against. It wasn't just a matter of a phone service, it was a matter of values.

This indifference highlights a broader issue within the church, a lack of understanding, or perhaps willful ignorance, of the power of consumer choices. Every dollar we spend is a vote. When we give our money to companies that stand against biblical values, we are in essence, supporting their agenda. Conversely, when we support companies like Patriot Mobile, we are voting for a society that upholds our values.

In "The Christian Wallet" by Mike Slaughter, this very issue is laid bare. Slaughter argues that christians have a moral obligation to spend their money in ways that reflect their faith. He points out that every dollar a christian spends has the potential to support either righteousness or unrighteousness, and too often, we unwittingly support the latter because it's more convenient. He challenges christians to "vote with their wallets" by supporting businesses that align with their faith, like Patriot Mobile, and boycotting those that do not.

Similarly, in "Faith Based Investing" by Tom McKissick, the author emphasizes that christians can make a profound impact simply by choosing where they spend and invest their money. He writes about the importance of "moral spending", a concept that encourages believers to put their financial support behind companies that align with biblical values. McKissick stresses that every time we choose to buy a product or use a service, we are making an ethical decision. It's not just about convenience or price, it's about making choices that reflect our core beliefs.

This sentiment is echoed in "Conscious Capitalism" by John Mackey, which, while not faith based, focuses on the power of consumers to change society by supporting companies that operate with higher ethical standards. The premise is simple, if christians and consumers in general shift their spending to businesses that align with their values, they can create real societal change. The key is intentionality, which is sadly lacking in many churches today.

When I reflect on these interactions with my fellow church members, I realize just how disconnected and indifferent the church has become from society and our culture. The church is called to be a force for good in this world, yet we so often fail to see how our everyday choices, like the phone companies we support, either build up or tear down the kingdom of God. If we continue to shrug off the importance of these decisions, then we are complicit in the advancement of the very ideologies we claim to oppose.

The lesson is clear, christians cannot afford to be indifferent about where their money goes. The church has the power to reshape society, but only if we choose to spend, invest, and live in a way that reflects the values we claim to hold dear. Otherwise, we are simply financing our own moral defeat.

David Daleiden: Exposing the Truth About Planned Parenthood

David Daleiden is a pro life activist and investigative journalist who made national headlines for his undercover work exposing Planned Parenthood's involvement in the sale of fetal tissue. Through the Center for Medical Progress, Daleiden and his team released a series of undercover videos showing Planned Parenthood executives discussing the sale of aborted baby parts for research, which sparked a national outcry and led to multiple investigations.

Despite facing legal battles and personal attacks, Daleiden has remained steadfast in his mission to expose the horrors of the abortion industry. His work has not only raised awareness about the practices of Planned Parenthood but has also helped galvanize the pro life movement, leading to legislative efforts to defund the organization and tighten regulations on abortion providers.

Daleiden's courage in the face of adversity is an example of what one person, armed with the truth, can accomplish. His willingness to risk his reputation and personal safety to uncover the truth about one of the most controversial issues in America serves as an inspiration to all Christians to stand boldly for life, no matter the cost.

Jack Phillips: Standing for Religious Freedom

Jack Phillips, the owner of Masterpiece Cakeshop in Colorado, became a symbol for religious freedom when he refused to create a custom wedding cake for a same sex marriage, citing his christian beliefs. His decision led to a legal battle that went all the way to the U.S. Supreme Court, where Phillips won a narrow victory in 2018.

Phillips' case highlighted the growing tension between religious liberty and the cultural push for acceptance of same sex marriage. While the legal battle took a toll on Phillips' business and personal life, he stood firm in his convictions, refusing to compromise his deeply held beliefs, even under immense pressure.

Phillips' story is a reminder that christians are increasingly being asked to choose between their faith and compliance with societal norms that contradict biblical teachings. His courageous stand for religious freedom is an example of the kind of boldness that is needed in the face of cultural pressure, and it serves as a rallying cry for other christians to defend their right to live out their faith publicly.

In the book "The Cost of My Faith: How a Decision in My Cake Shop Took Me to the Supreme Court" by Jack Phillips, he shares a deeply personal and powerful account of what he went through as a result of standing up for his religious beliefs. Phillips recounts the day in 2012 when a same sex couple came into his Masterpiece Cakeshop and asked him to create a custom wedding cake for their marriage. When Jack politely declined, offering to sell them any other item in his store, he had no idea that his life would soon become a national spectacle.

He writes about the immediate backlash that followed, including the vitriolic response from the media, local activists, and even former customers. Phillips describes the anguish of being labeled a bigot and a homophobe, despite his sincere efforts to treat every customer with dignity and respect. In his words, the media's portrayal of him as a villain "felt like a tidal wave crashing down, threatening to sweep everything I had worked for away in an instant."

What began as a simple decision to follow his faith led to legal battles that stretched over six years, with Phillips facing multiple lawsuits, including one filed by the Colorado Civil Rights Commission. He details the financial and emotional toll that these battles took on his family and his business. With threats, protests, and calls for boycotts, the small cake shop became a battleground for what Phillips describes as the fight for religious liberty in America.

Phillips also writes about the immense pressure he felt to give in, to settle the case or to compromise on his beliefs for the sake of his livelihood and peace of mind. However, his faith and conviction would not allow him to do so. He shares how prayer and his belief in God's plan for his life sustained him during the darkest moments, and how legal organizations like Alliance Defending Freedom stepped in to help him fight this legal battle all the way to the supreme court.

The turning point came when his case reached the U.S. Supreme Court in 2017. Phillips vividly describes the anxiety of waiting for the decision, knowing that the outcome would not just affect him, but would set a precedent for other christians and business owners across the country.

When the court ruled 7-2 in his favor in 2018, finding that the Colorado Civil Rights Commission had shown hostility towards his religious beliefs, Phillips knew it was a major victory, but his fight wasn't over.

Even after the ruling, Phillips faced continued legal challenges and societal pressure, as other customers brought lawsuits against him for refusing to create cakes with messages that conflicted with his beliefs. He describes this ongoing battle as one that tested the limits of his endurance but ultimately strengthened his faith. Through it all, Phillips maintains that the case was never about denying service to anyone, it was about the right to live out his faith in his work without being compelled to participate in something that violated his conscience.

Phillips' story is a testimony to the cost of standing up for one's beliefs in an increasingly hostile cultural climate. His journey illustrates the real world consequences of religious conviction and the price of adhering to principles that are deeply rooted in faith, even when the world pushes back.

Abby Johnson: From Planned Parenthood to Pro Life Advocate

Abby Johnson was once a director of a Planned Parenthood clinic and a staunch advocate of abortion rights. However, her life changed dramatically when she witnessed an ultrasound guided abortion, which led her to leave the abortion industry and become one of the most outspoken pro life advocates in the country.

Johnson's story, chronicled in her memoir Unplanned and the subsequent film adaptation, has inspired thousands of people to join the fight to end abortion. Today, she leads And Then There Were None, a ministry dedicated to helping abortion clinic workers leave the industry and find healing and restoration.

Johnson's conversion from abortion advocate to pro life warrior illustrates the power of God's grace to transform even the most unlikely individuals. Her testimony is a reminder that no one is beyond redemption and that the most powerful voices in any movement are often those who have experienced a radical change of heart.

While individuals like those mentioned above are making a significant impact, they are part of a larger movement of believers who understand that the church must be actively engaged in the cultural and political battles of our time. The church is not called to retreat into the shadows but to stand as a light in the darkness, Matthew 5:14-16.

This chapter closes by examining how churches across the nation are beginning to awaken to the need for collective action. From local pastors organizing prayer marches to congregations mobilizing to support pro family legislation, the body of Christ is rising up to meet the challenges of our day.

The people profiled in this chapter are not extraordinary because of their circumstances, resources, or abilities. What makes them remarkable is their willingness to take a stand when it would have been easier to remain silent. They have answered the call to make a difference, even when it comes at great personal cost.

Their stories challenge each of us to ask, What can I do to make a difference? Whether through advocacy, activism, prayer, or simply supporting those on the front lines, every christian has a role to play in the fight for truth and justice. Now is the time for the church to raise its voice and take action, following the example of those who have courageously led the way.

The world needs more people who are willing to stand for what is right, no matter the cost. Will you be one of them?

CHAPTER 12 :

God's Restraining Force

You know, I've been thinking about how incredible it is that words hold so much power. The Bible even says, "Life and death are in the power of the tongue." Words can build up, or they can destroy, and it's not just a spiritual truth, but something we see playing out every day. Yet, what really boggles my mind is how the most ridiculous, outright destructive ideas, ideas that are easily disprovable, are somehow still making inroads into people's minds, especially in schools.

I mean, think about it. We've got Marxist ideologies being subtly or not so subtly, inserted into curriculums, and the scary part is, they're being accepted as if they're just another harmless perspective. How do they do it? Words. Just words, but they use them so well. Terms like "equity" or "social justice" sound great on the surface, who wouldn't want fairness or justice? But dig a little deeper, and you quickly realize those words are masking something much darker. And yet, these ideas take root because, let's face it, words have power. A slick, well phrased lie is sometimes more powerful than an uncomfortable truth.

The Bible knew this long before we were watching school boards across the country embrace nonsense. Life and death are literally in the power of the tongue. Marxists seem to understand that better than most christians do. They take their ideology, wrap it up in the right words, and next thing you know, it's being taught as fact in classrooms. "Hey kids, capitalism is bad, families are oppressive, and gender is just a construct." Right. Makes perfect sense, doesn't it?

The irony is, the ideas they're spreading are so blatantly bad that it's hard to comprehend how anyone could actually buy into them. But there it is, and people do. We've got young minds swallowing this stuff whole, and not just in the universities anymore. It's trickling down into elementary schools. They're actually teaching kids that men can be women, and women can be men, and that's just "progress." And somehow, parents, teachers, even many in the church are just watching it happen, as if words don't matter.

But they do matter, and we see it every day. These words shape reality. You and I both know, if you repeat a lie often enough, people start believing it. And that's exactly what's happening. They're feeding kids these false narratives, repeating them until they're ingrained in their minds. It doesn't matter if it's obviously wrong, if you hear it enough times, you start to accept it as truth. And the scary part is, that's all it takes to shift an entire generation. Just words.

Honestly, it's like watching the emperor parade around in his "new clothes," and the masses are all nodding in approval. "Yes, of course, gender doesn't matter. Yes, of course, men can give birth." Sure. Why not? Let's just throw out thousands of years of biology while we're at it.

And the thing is, it's not that these people haven't heard the truth. The truth is out there, clear as day. But there's a kind of power in a lie that's been repeated over and over, especially when it's wrapped up in fancy, high minded terms. People start thinking, "Well, maybe there's something to this after all." Even when their own common sense is screaming at them that it's garbage. I mean, just look at the results. Schools are turning out kids who can barely read or do math, but they've got all the latest buzzwords down pat. They can tell you all about "gender fluidity" and "systemic oppression." Brilliant.

What's baffling is that christians, of all people, should be the ones who understand the power of words. We've got the Bible, which is full of warnings about being careful with what we say. Jesus himself said, "Out of the abundance of the heart the mouth speaks." If that's not a call to guard our words and pay attention to the language we use, I don't know what is. But instead of using our words to push back against these lies, too many christians are just staying silent. Or worse, they're adopting the language of the world and going along with it.

It's like they've forgotten that our words have creative power. If we speak the truth, we have the power to change hearts and minds, to bring life where there's been death. But if we stay silent, we're letting the enemy use his words to destroy. And make no mistake, that's exactly what's happening right now. This flood of bad ideas, these Marxist ideologies, they're not just harmless words. They're shaping the future and it's not looking pretty.

It's hard to believe that something so obviously wrong could still hold sway, but here we are. It just proves what the Bible says, words carry power. Whether we use them for good or evil, they have the ability to shape the world around us. We can't afford to be careless with that. The church needs to wake up and start speaking truth again before it's too late.

In a world that seems to be descending into chaos and moral decay, it can be easy to forget the vital role that God's people, His Church, play in restraining the forces of evil. Scripture makes it clear that the presence of the righteous has a powerful effect on the world around them. It is through the prayers, actions, and influence of believers that evil is often held at bay, and society is prevented from spiraling into complete moral and spiritual collapse.

This chapter explores the concept of God's restraining force. How the church is called to act as a spiritual barrier against the advancement of wickedness. It delves into the biblical principles that illustrate the power of God's people in shaping the destiny of nations and how their presence, prayers, and actions can either delay or accelerate the downfall of a society.

In Matthew 5:13-16, Jesus calls His followers the "salt of the earth" and the "light of the world." These metaphors hold deep significance for understanding the role of the church as God's restraining force.

In the ancient world, salt was used primarily as a preservative, preventing the decay of food. Similarly, the church is meant to act as a preservative in society, slowing the spread of moral decay. Salt also adds flavor, just as the church should bring the light of truth and goodness to an otherwise tasteless, corrupt world. When the church is active in its mission, it preserves what is good and prevents the complete corruption of society.

Light reveals what is hidden in darkness. As the light of the world, the church exposes the evil that seeks to hide in the shadows. The church's responsibility is to bring truth to light, exposing lies, injustice, and immorality, and pointing people toward the righteousness of God.

When the church fails to be salt and light, society suffers. Without the restraining presence of the righteous, evil is given free rein to spread unchecked. This is why it is critical for believers to remain engaged, active, and vocal in their communities and in the world at large.

Second Thessalonians 2:6-7 speaks of a "restrainer" who holds back the full force of evil until the appointed time. While scholars debate the specific identity of the restrainer, many believe this passage refers to the Holy Spirit, working through the church to restrain the power of lawlessness in the world.

The Holy Spirit indwells every believer, empowering them to live godly lives and to stand against the tide of sin. As long as the church is present on earth, the Holy Spirit works through God's people to limit the advance of evil. It is the combined effect of millions of christians, praying, serving, and witnessing, that keeps society from plunging into utter darkness.

However, this restraint will not last forever. According to 2 Thessalonians, there will come a time when the restraining force is removed, allowing the full force of lawlessness to manifest. This points to a future time of great tribulation, but until then, the church must continue to fulfill its role as God's restraining force.

One of the most significant ways the church acts as a restraining force is through prayer. Scripture is filled with examples of how the prayers of the righteous have the power to hold back judgment and protect nations from destruction.

Abraham's Intercession for Sodom In Genesis 18, Abraham intercedes with God on behalf of Sodom and Gomorrah, asking God to spare the city if even ten righteous people can be found. While the cities were ultimately destroyed due to their wickedness, Abraham's prayer shows that the presence of the righteous could have delayed or even prevented their judgment.

Moses' Prayer for Israel, In Exodus 32, after the Israelites sinned by worshiping the golden calf, God was ready to destroy the entire nation. But Moses interceded on their behalf, and God relented. This demonstrates the power of one righteous person's prayer in staying God's hand of judgment.

Daniel's Prayer for His People In Daniel 9, Daniel prays for the restoration of Israel after they had been in exile due to their disobedience. His prayer of repentance on behalf of his people led to God's promise of restoration and deliverance.

The church today has the same opportunity to intercede for its nation, communities, and the world. In a time of increasing darkness, the prayers of the righteous are a powerful force in holding back evil and delaying God's judgment. When the church fails to pray, it abdicates one of its most critical responsibilities as God's restraining force.

The church's role as a restraining force is not limited to spiritual matters alone. It also involves taking a stand against cultural and moral decline. Throughout history, the church has played a crucial role in confronting injustice, protecting the vulnerable, and challenging societal norms that violate God's moral law.

Many of the leaders of the abolitionist movement were devout christians who believed that slavery was a moral evil that needed to be eradicated. Their activism, fueled by their faith, was instrumental in bringing about the end of slavery in the Western world.

The American civil rights movement was led by christian pastors and laypeople who were committed to the biblical principles of justice and equality. They understood that their faith called them to confront the systemic racism and injustice of their time.

Today, the pro life movement is driven largely by christians who believe that every life is sacred and made in the image of God. Their efforts have led to significant legal battles, the closure of abortion clinics, and a growing cultural awareness of the value of life.

The church must continue to speak out against the moral evils of our time, whether it be abortion, human trafficking, or the erosion of religious freedom. When the church remains silent in the face of evil, it allows the forces of darkness to gain ground. But when believers stand up for what is right, they act as God's restraining force, pushing back against the moral collapse of society.

In the book "The Cost of Our Silence, Consequences Of Christians Taking the Path of Least Resistance" by David Fiorazo, he provides a compelling critique of how the church has become increasingly passive in the face of significant moral and political challenges. Fiorazo argues that instead of being the bold, prophetic voice that speaks out against evil, the church has largely chosen comfort over confrontation. This silence, he claims, has come at a steep price, not just for the church but for society as a whole. By avoiding uncomfortable conversations and failing to challenge the dominant cultural narratives, the church has allowed moral decay to take root.

Fiorazo paints a picture of a church that has prioritized cultural acceptance over biblical conviction. He argues that many christians today have been seduced by the desire for societal approval and are unwilling to risk being labeled as intolerant or judgmental. The result is a church that has become irrelevant in the most critical cultural battles of our time. Fiorazo points out that by choosing not to speak out on issues like abortion, the sanctity of marriage, religious freedom, and the moral corruption of our political system, the church has effectively abandoned its responsibility to be the "salt and light" that Christ called it to be.

He emphasizes that silence is not neutrality, rather it's a form of complicity. Fiorazo explains that when the church remains silent in the face of evil, it is essentially giving its tacit approval. He uses the example of abortion, which he calls "the greatest moral evil of our time." Despite the fact that millions of innocent lives are being taken every year, many churches choose to stay silent on the issue because they fear alienating people or being seen as too political. Fiorazo warns that this silence will not only cost the church its moral authority, but it will also contribute to the further erosion of society's moral fabric.

In his view, the church's failure to speak out against the culture's growing acceptance of immorality has directly led to the breakdown of the family, the loss of religious freedoms, and the legalization of injustices like abortion and human trafficking. Fiorazo draws a direct line between the church's silence and the moral chaos that has taken over much of Western culture. He calls on christians to wake up and realize that their silence is not an act of love or tolerance, but a betrayal of the gospel.

Fiorazo isn't alone in his critique. In "The Cost of Discipleship" by Dietrich Bonhoeffer, the German theologian confronts a similar issue but from the perspective of Nazi Germany. Bonhoeffer was one of the few christian leaders who spoke out against Adolf Hitler and the atrocities of the Nazi regime. He condemned the German church for its cowardice, for turning a blind eye to the growing evil around it. Bonhoeffer's warnings about the cost of silence are as relevant today as they were in his time.

Bonhoeffer saw firsthand how the church's refusal to confront evil allowed one of the most brutal regimes in history to rise to power. He spoke against what he called "cheap grace", the idea that one could be a christian without making any sacrifices, without carrying the burden of standing up for what is right, even when it is unpopular. For Bonhoeffer, cheap grace was grace without discipleship, without the cross, and without any real cost. He believed that the church's silence in the face of evil was a clear indication that it had embraced cheap grace, and that such silence would ultimately lead to its downfall.

Both Bonhoeffer and Fiorazo make the argument that silence is not just a failure of moral courage, it is a failure of faith. To be silent in the face of injustice is to reject the call to follow Christ, who always spoke truth to power, even at great personal cost. Bonhoeffer famously joined a plot to assassinate Hitler, believing that it was not enough to simply oppose evil with words, sometimes action is necessary. He was eventually executed for his involvement in the resistance, but his legacy as a christian who refused to remain silent in the face of evil continues to inspire believers today.

Fiorazo extends Bonhoeffer's warning to the modern church, arguing that while the church may not be facing a tyrant like Hitler, it is nevertheless facing a growing tide of evil that must be confronted. Whether it is the issue of abortion, the attack on religious liberty, or the moral decay of the culture, the church cannot afford to remain silent. Fiorazo warns that if christians continue to take the path of least resistance, choosing to stay quiet to avoid conflict, they will not only lose their moral authority, but they will also lose their freedoms.

He challenges christians to look at the example of those who came before, like Bonhoeffer, and to realize that the cost of discipleship is not optional.

The gospel requires believers to speak out against evil, even when it is uncomfortable or unpopular. He points out that throughout history, the church has often been at its strongest when it has been willing to stand up to the culture, to challenge the status quo, and to confront evil head on. But when the church chooses silence, it not only abdicates its responsibility, it also becomes complicit in the very evils it claims to oppose.

In "Letter to the American Church" by Eric Metaxas, another book that draws inspiration from Bonhoeffer's legacy, Metaxas directly compares the American church today to the German church during the rise of Hitler. He warns that the same complacency and fear that paralyzed the German church in the 1930s is now infecting the American church. Metaxas argues that if the church does not find its voice soon, it will face the same consequences as the German church did, and ultimately in the downfall of the nation.

The message from Fiorazo, Bonhoeffer, and Metaxas is clear, the church must wake up. The path of least resistance, the path of silence leads to destruction, not only for the church but for society as a whole. As the moral decay continues to spread, the church's voice is needed now more than ever. It must speak out against the cultural, moral, and political issues that are eroding the foundations of civilization. If the church fails to do this, it will not only lose its influence but also its very purpose.

For those who claim that the church should stay out of politics, Fiorazo and Bonhoeffer offer a stark warning, silence in the face of evil is not an option for followers of Christ. The cost of silence is too great, both for the church and for the world. The time has come for christians to stand up, speak out, and be the light in the darkness. The future of the church, and of society itself depends on it.

CHAPTER 13

Up, Up, And Away

Before I begin this chapter, I must point out that the idea of the rapture, at least the way it's commonly understood today, didn't really become mainstream until the 19th and 20th centuries.

The truth is, the modern version of the rapture, where christians are plucked from the earth before any tribulation occurs, is largely credited to a man named John Nelson Darby in the early 1800s. Darby, a British evangelist and founder of the Plymouth Brethren, is widely regarded as the father of modern dispensationalism. He popularized the idea of a "secret rapture" in which believers would be taken up to heaven before the world plunged into a period of great suffering, known as the tribulation. But here's the catch, this idea wasn't exactly a prevailing interpretation of scripture prior to Darby's time.

For most of church history, christians didn't anticipate escaping the world's troubles, they fully expected to endure them. The early church certainly didn't believe they'd be whisked away to avoid persecution, they lived through persecution. Many were martyred, tortured, and exiled for their faith, and they saw these tribulations as part and parcel of what it meant to follow Christ. Their hope wasn't in escaping hardship but in Christ's return at the end of history to judge the world and establish His kingdom. The rapture, as popularly conceived today, would've been a foreign concept to them.

It wasn't until Darby's teachings spread, particularly through the work of the Scofield Reference Bible in the early 20th century, that the rapture began to capture the imagination of modern christians, especially in America. The Scofield Bible, with its extensive dispensational notes, introduced this, "rapture before tribulation" doctrine to an entire generation of readers. Soon, it became the dominant eschatological, end times belief in many evangelical circles.

And, let's be honest, the idea of being pulled out of a world spiraling into chaos is a bit of a convenient theology. Who wouldn't want to believe that just before everything gets really bad, we'll all be "up, up, and away," safely removed from the mess down here? But this has led to passivity in most churches in the free world, it's a mindset that says, "Why bother engaging in the world's problems when we won't be here to deal with the consequences? Let the world burn, we're getting out of here."

But here's the kicker, this mindset ignores centuries of christian teaching that emphasized endurance, perseverance, and the call to be salt and light in the world. It also overlooks the many biblical passages that call believers to be active participants in God's work on earth, not bystanders waiting for an escape plan. The early church didn't check out and wait for rescue, they actively resisted the world's evil, even when it cost them everything.

So, before we dive further into this discussion, let's be clear, the rapture as we understand it today is a relatively recent theological development. It's a modern idea, shaped more by 19th century eschatology than by the teachings of Christ or the apostles. It has certainly taken root in the American church, but it's worth questioning whether it's made us less engaged, less concerned with the moral decay around us, and less willing to fight the battles we're called to fight. After all, if we're all just waiting to be swept away, why bother taking a stand? And that, my friends, is exactly the kind of thinking that's helping to bring about the very collapse we're supposedly so eager to avoid.

A troubling mentality has taken root in the Western church. It's the belief that we won't experience real suffering or turmoil here because, when things get bad enough, the rapture will whisk us away. It's become more than a theological position, it's an excuse to stay disengaged from the cultural and societal issues unfolding around us. Why bother confronting injustice when we think we won't be here long enough to see the consequences? But while most of us overweight people in the west sit in comfortable sanctuaries sipping our coffee and waiting for escape, believers in places like Nigeria, North Korea, and China are living in great tribulation.

In these countries, following Christ isn't a Sunday inconvenience, it's often a death sentence. Christians are being imprisoned, beheaded, raped, starved, ostracized, and hanged. Their homes are burned, property stolen, and their lives reduced to unimaginable suffering. And this isn't some distant future prophecy. It's happening right now, and of course we rarely hear this from the pulpit. While we enjoy our freedoms, many believers around the world are enduring hell on earth every day.

When I mentioned this reality to a pastor recently, his response was, "Well, at least it's not the great tribulation." I was stunned. How disconnected can someone be to say that? How could a future tribulation possibly be worse for believers who are already being brutalized and killed? What version of suffering are we waiting for that would finally motivate us to care?

This mindset reveals how out of touch many christians in the free world have become. It's easier to wait for divine evacuation than to engage with the suffering of others. But Jesus never told us to stand on the sidelines and wait for rescue. He told us to take up our cross, fight for justice, and love sacrificially, no matter how hard the world gets.

The Bible is clear that while believers are called to eagerly await Christ's return, they are also called to be active, vigilant, and engaged in the world until that day comes, Luke 19:13.

The problem with the "up, up, and away" mindset is that it fosters a false sense of security. Christians who adopt this perspective often disengage from societal issues, thinking that their primary role is simply to "hold on" until Christ returns. This mindset can lead to several negative outcomes.

If believers are only concerned with escaping the world, they are less likely to care about the injustices happening around them. Issues like abortion, human trafficking, illegal immigration, and religious persecution can be ignored if christians believe they will soon be taken away from it all.

Many christians avoid participating in politics or culture because they see such efforts as futile. They reason that since the world is destined to get worse, there is no point in trying to change it. This withdrawal leaves a vacuum for secular ideologies to dominate, further accelerating moral decline.

The Great Commission, Matthew 28:19-20 commands believers to make disciples of all nations, teaching them to observe all that Christ commanded. However, an escapist mindset often leads to a neglect of this mission. If the focus is solely on escaping the world, there is little motivation to engage with it, much less reach the lost and make disciples.

This chapter warns against the dangers of this mindset, showing how it undermines the church's ability to be salt and light in the world, Matthew 5:13-16 and how it prevents christians from fulfilling their God given responsibilities.

The Bible teaches a clear balance between hopeful anticipation of Christ's return and active engagement in the world. Jesus Himself spoke about His second coming, but He never suggested that His followers should sit back and wait for it passively. Instead, He gave numerous parables and teachings that emphasize the importance of being faithful stewards, working diligently until He returns.

The Parable of the Talents, Matthew 25:14-30. In this parable, a master gives his servants talents to manage while he is away. The servants who invested and multiplied their talents were praised, while the servant who buried his talent in fear and inactivity was condemned. This parable teaches that believers are expected to use their gifts and resources to further God's kingdom on earth, not hide them away while waiting for Christ's return.

Occupy Until He Comes, Luke 19:13. In this passage, Jesus instructs His followers to "occupy" or "do business" until He comes back. This is a clear call for believers to remain engaged and active in the world, fulfilling their responsibilities and making an impact until He returns.

 Christians are called to shine as lights in a dark and perverse generation. This implies active engagement with the world, not retreat. Believers are to live out their faith in such a way that it impacts the world around them, demonstrating the love, truth, and justice of God.

These passages, and many others, make it clear that christians are to remain faithful and diligent in their work for the Kingdom, regardless of when Christ will return.

When christians adopt an escapist mindset, the effects on society can be devastating. The church is meant to be a restraining force against evil, as discussed in the previous chapter, and when it withdraws from that role, evil is allowed to spread unchecked.

When christians disengage from cultural and political life, they leave a void that is quickly filled by secular ideologies. This has contributed to the rapid moral decline we see in areas like the sexual revolution, the rise of abortion, and the erosion of religious freedom.

The church once played a significant role in shaping public policy, particularly in areas of justice, education, and care for the vulnerable. However, as christians have retreated from the political sphere, secular voices have dominated, leading to policies that often conflict with biblical values.

When christians are absent from the fight for justice, it is the most vulnerable who suffer. Whether it's the unborn, victims of human trafficking, or those persecuted for their faith, the church's inaction has real and devastating consequences for those in need of protection and advocacy.

This chapter illustrates that the church's withdrawal has far reaching consequences, not only for society at large but for the church itself. When believers fail to engage, they lose their prophetic voice and miss the opportunity to be a force for good in the world.

While christians are right to look forward to the return of Christ with eager anticipation, they must also recognize that they have a mission to fulfill in the here and now. The Bible is clear that this world will face trials and tribulations, but that doesn't excuse believers from the responsibility of working for justice, sharing the gospel, and standing up for truth.

Rather than retreating, christians should see themselves as ambassadors of Christ, 2 Corinthians 5:20, representing His kingdom on earth and working to influence culture for the better. Whether through politics, education, business, or art, christians are called to be active participants in the world, shaping it according to God's principles.

The hope of Christ's return should motivate christians to live holy, impactful lives, not cause them to disengage. In fact, the knowledge that time is short should inspire greater urgency in sharing the gospel, fighting for justice, and being a force for good in a fallen world.

Jesus' return will be sudden and unexpected, but believers are called to be faithful in the meantime. This means using our time, talents, and resources to further God's kingdom and make a difference in the world, trusting that our efforts are not in vain, 1 Corinthians 15:58.

The "up, up, and away" mindset may offer a comforting sense of escape, but it ultimately leads to a failure in the church's mission. As believers, we are called to be actively engaged in the world, not withdrawing into a bubble of self preservation. Christ's return is certain, but until that day comes, the church has work to do.

This chapter calls christians to reject the false comfort of escapism and instead embrace the call to be God's hands and feet in the world. By balancing a hopeful expectation of Christ's return with a deep sense of responsibility to live out our faith now, we can fulfill the mission God has given us and make a lasting impact on the world around us.

CHAPTER 14

Warnings For America

In examining the state of America through a biblical worldview, we can see two contrasting groups. The first group comprises of individuals actively working to push destructive policies and ideas. These are the people championing agendas such as the normalization of transgender ideology, including irreversible surgeries on minors, and promoting heavy government control that limits individual freedom. They are relentless. They show up to vote in every election. They flood social media, making their voices heard in every possible venue. Whether times are good or bad, they remain unwavering in their pursuit to advance their agenda. To them, there's no off season in the battle for cultural and political dominance. Their dedication is undeniable, and frightening.

This group stands in stark contrast to another segment of society, including many within the church. These individuals neither endorse wicked policies nor seek to actively prevent them. They may have good intentions but live comfortably removed from the political and cultural battles raging around them. They talk about how bad the world is getting, often acknowledging its moral decline in private conversations. But for most, that's all it is, just talk. There is no sense of urgency or personal responsibility to engage in meaningful action.

A conversation I had with a christian man, let's call him Bill, but that's not his real name. Bill perfectly illustrates this mindset. Bill is well aware of the world's increasing wickedness, but rather than feeling compelled to act, he finds solace in it. "The worse things get," Bill told me, "the more hopeful I become." His reasoning? He believes that worsening conditions signal the imminent return of Jesus Christ. While I understand the eschatological hope in Christ's return, this mindset deeply troubles me. It overlooks the real suffering happening in the present. Unborn babies are being slaughtered in their mothers' wombs. Young children are being sterilized and mutilated under the guise of "affirming care." The nation itself is disintegrating from within, yet Bill remains passive, at peace with the chaos because it hasn't touched him directly.

Bill may vote, but he does so without anger or urgency. His sense of hope blinds him to the immediate need for action. The problem is, that people like Bill only seem to care when their comfort is threatened. They don't engage when others suffer, but I suspect that when bad policies finally hit home, their perspective will shift dramatically. When retirement funds dry up, when food and fuel shortages impact their lives, and when chaos shows up at their own front doors, only then will they awaken.

By then, the conversation will change. Bill won't be joyful about the state of the world anymore. When the comforts he relied on are gone, when the world he ignored begins to encroach on his personal peace, he'll have what you might call a "come to reality" moment. It's easy to dismiss evil when it's happening to others, far harder when it invades your life.

As America stands at a cultural and political crossroads, there are numerous warnings that echo from both history and present day experiences around the world. These warnings serve as flashing red lights, urging America to stop, reflect, and change course before it is too late. Nations that have fallen into tyranny, moral decay, or economic collapse often share eerily similar trajectories, trajectories that America, if it continues on its current path, is dangerously close to following.

This chapter examines the lessons that can be drawn from the fall of other great nations and the urgent warnings coming from those who have already walked the path that America is now on. It is a sobering look at the parallels between America's current condition and the mistakes made by nations that once enjoyed freedom, prosperity, and influence but fell to internal corruption, external threats, or both. Most importantly, it serves as a clarion call for the church in America to wake up, take these warnings seriously, and act as a force for repentance and change.

You know, if christians in communist countries had a chance to sit down and really understand the state of the church in the free world today, they'd probably be shocked and heartbroken. They've lived through regimes where practicing their faith, or even speaking truth to power, could land them in prison or worse. And yet, despite all that oppression, they've been some of the most vocal about standing up for what's right, about calling out evil when they see it, even when it means putting their lives on the line. They know what it means to live under a government that suppresses their voice and destroys the moral fabric of society.

Now imagine if they learned that the church in the free world, where we have the luxury to speak, to vote, and to gather without fear, is largely silent on these issues. That instead of using its influence to speak truth to power, the church is mostly retreating behind excuses like "God is in control" or "this world is not my home." You and I both know that while those statements are true on a theological level, they're often just used as a cop out for not engaging with the messiness of politics and society. How would those christians, who have risked their lives to follow Christ, feel about that?

I bet they'd be appalled. I can picture them saying, "We fought for our faith under regimes that tried to silence us, and you, in the free world, who have the ability to stand up and make a difference, do nothing?" It's not even that the church in the free world is just staying neutral. By staying silent, they're effectively allowing the moral decline to continue unchecked. They're passively contributing to the societal decay that comes when we don't stand up for biblical principles in the public square.

It's almost like a betrayal. These christians who have been persecuted for their faith would likely feel abandoned by their brothers and sisters in the West, as if the Western church doesn't value the freedoms they still have. And while they've had to live under dictatorships or oppressive regimes, the church in the West has watched as our own political systems become more and more corrupt, more hostile to christian values, and done little about it.

The saddest part? Most of these Western christians don't even realize it. They've been lulled into this false sense of security that says, "Well, we don't have to engage with this world because we're just passing through." But in communist countries, christians know that kind of thinking is dangerous. They've seen what happens when the church disengages from politics, evil flourishes, and the people suffer.

I imagine those persecuted christians would say, "How could you stand by while your society crumbles around you? How could you not raise your voice when there's still time?" They know that if you don't speak out, if you don't push back against evil, it only grows stronger. And what's terrifying is that they'd recognize the early signs of oppression in the free world long before most Western christians even noticed.

And that's exactly the point. Those who've lived through oppression see the warning signs in the West, but they're shouting into a void. They're warning us, but we're too busy with our comforts, our petty disagreements, or our desire to stay "above" politics to listen. If they had the freedoms we have here, they wouldn't squander them. They'd be on the front lines of the fight, speaking truth, even if it made them unpopular or uncomfortable.

What do you think about that? Because to me, it seems like christians in the free world are wasting an opportunity that persecuted christians can only dream of. And the stakes are so high. Our silence today is laying the groundwork for our own future oppression. We're basically giving the enemy a free pass by refusing to engage. Meanwhile, our brothers and sisters in Christ are still fighting, still suffering under regimes that have perfected the art of silencing the church. If we don't wake up, we might soon find ourselves in a similar situation.

In the book "Live Not by Lies, A Manual for Christian Dissidents" by Rod Dreher, the author offers a dire warning to Americans based on the testimonies of people who survived the brutal realities of Soviet totalitarianism. Dreher emphasizes that many of these survivors are sounding the alarm because they see troubling parallels between the rise of soft totalitarianism in the U.S. and the early days of communist regimes in Eastern Europe and the Soviet Union. Unlike hard totalitarianism, where the state imposes its will through violent repression, soft totalitarianism is more insidious. It works through manipulation, cultural pressure, the suppression of free speech, and ideological conformity. It creeps in quietly, often disguised as progress or social justice, but its effects are no less devastating.

In the testimonies Dreher gathered, people describe how their societies slowly gave way to authoritarian rule not through dramatic military coups, but through the gradual erosion of individual liberties. People were forced to publicly conform to lies they didn't believe in, whether it was about the superiority of the state, the abolition of religion, or the glorification of communist leaders. This public conformity, Dreher explains, is already happening in America, where speaking out against the prevailing ideologies, whether on issues like gender, race, or politics, can result in social and professional ostracization. The dissidents warn that once a society begins to accept lies and punishes those who speak the truth, it's already on a path toward totalitarian control. Dreher describes how those who resisted in communist regimes often did so at great personal cost, and he argues that the time to resist in America is now, before the consequences become as severe as they did in the former Soviet states.

One powerful example Dreher cites comes from a Soviet dissident who described how the state controlled every aspect of life by making people afraid to speak their minds, afraid to worship freely, and afraid to live according to their own consciences. This fear, the dissident said, allowed the government to enforce ideological conformity without needing to resort to overt violence. Dreher warns that Americans are already being conditioned to live in fear, fear of being canceled, fear of losing their jobs, fear of being labeled a bigot or extremist. He argues that if Americans don't recognize and resist this cultural shift, they will find themselves living under a regime of ideological control every bit as oppressive as the Soviet system.

In "The Devil and Karl Marx, Communism's Long March of Death, Deception, and Infiltration", Paul Kengor delves deep into the history of Marxist ideology, showing how it infiltrates and ultimately destroys societies from within. Kengor warns that the same Marxist principles that ravaged nations like Russia and China are now finding a foothold in America under the guise of progressive activism. He details how communist revolutions throughout history did not simply overthrow governments but dismantled the very fabric of society, family structures, religious institutions, and individual rights were all targets. Marxism, Kengor explains, was never just about economics, it was about reshaping society to fit a godless, collectivist vision, where the state replaces religion and individual freedom is sacrificed for the "greater good."

Kengor highlights how, throughout history, Marxist movements have always begun by targeting the youth, using educational institutions to indoctrinate the next generation. This, he warns, is already happening in American universities, where students are being taught to reject traditional American values, demonize capitalism, and embrace radical social and economic ideologies. He draws comparisons between this and the early days of the Bolshevik Revolution, where intellectual elites in Russia first spread Marxist ideas in universities, preparing the way for the revolution that would lead to decades of suffering, poverty, and repression.

One of the most chilling parallels Kengor draws is between the way Marxist regimes used propaganda to control public opinion and the way today's media, social platforms, and educational systems in the U.S. enforce ideological conformity. In communist regimes, the media was used to push the party line, suppress dissent, and rewrite history. Today, Kengor argues, many mainstream media outlets and tech platforms are doing something eerily similar, promoting a narrow set of acceptable views on topics like gender, race, and politics while censoring or deplatforming those who dare to dissent. This control of information, Kengor warns, is a hallmark of totalitarianism, and unless it is resisted, it will lead to the same kind of societal collapse that happened in communist countries.

In "The Naked Communist", W. Cleon Skousen offers another stark warning to America. Skousen outlines the long term strategy of communist ideologies, showing how they infiltrate from within, using cultural institutions to weaken a nation's resolve. He lists 45 specific communist goals that were revealed in the 1950s, many of which have already come to pass in America. These goals include breaking down the family unit, weakening religious influence, taking control of the media, and infiltrating the education system. Skousen argues that these goals were not about revolution through violence but about revolution through cultural subversion, gradually eroding the pillars of Western society until it collapses under its own weight.

Skousen's warnings are particularly relevant today, as Americans face increasing pressure to abandon traditional values in favor of a new story of progressive orthodoxy. He points to the breakdown of the family as one of the most dangerous trends in modern America, showing how communist regimes always sought to replace the family with the state, turning children into wards of the government. Today, Skousen argues, the family is under attack in the U.S., not through overt government intervention but through social and cultural forces that devalue marriage, encourage divorce, and promote alternative family structures. He warns that if Americans don't stand up for the family, they will lose one of the most important defenses against totalitarian control.

In all these books, the message is clear, America is on a dangerous path, and the warning signs are all too familiar to those who have lived through the horrors of communist regimes. These authors plead with Americans to recognize the signs before it's too late and to take action to preserve the freedoms that are being eroded. The warning is stark, once freedom is lost, it is incredibly difficult to regain. These books serve as a powerful reminder that the cost of silence, compliance, and inaction can be devastating for a nation and its people.

Throughout history, many empires and nations that once stood strong and proud have collapsed from within due to moral decay, political corruption, and the erosion of core values. The Roman Empire is a prime example. At its height, Rome was the most powerful empire in the world, but over time, internal corruption, complacency, and a loss of moral compass led to its downfall. The moral degradation of society, an unresponsive government, and a decline in civic duty all contributed to Rome's collapse.

America is not immune to these same forces. Like Rome, America has been a symbol of freedom, democracy, and strength. But just like Rome, America is showing signs of internal decay. Warnings from history remind us that nations do not fall overnight, they fall gradually as they abandon the principles and values that made them great. The Roman Empire collapsed not just because of external threats, but because it rotted from within. If America is not careful, it could follow the same path.

Warnings from Cuba and Venezuela: The Perils of Socialism

In recent years, many who fled oppressive regimes have raised warnings about America's flirtation with socialism. The stories of Cuba and Venezuela are particularly poignant. Both countries were once thriving, Cuba was one of the wealthiest nations in Latin America, and Venezuela was one of the richest oil producing countries in the world. Yet both nations are now mired in poverty, oppression, and economic ruin after turning toward socialism.

When Fidel Castro took power in 1959, Cuba was transformed into a socialist state under the guise of creating equality and prosperity for all. Instead, the government stripped away individual freedoms, private property, and free enterprise. Today Cuba remains a cautionary tale of how quickly a prosperous nation can descend into authoritarianism and poverty under socialism. Those who have fled Cuba warn that America is teetering on the edge of embracing similar policies, which could lead to the same disastrous results.

Venezuela's downfall was even more rapid. In the early 2000s, under Hugo Chávez, the government began nationalizing industries and implementing widespread socialist policies. These policies quickly led to the collapse of Venezuela's economy, causing hyperinflation, mass poverty, and food shortages. Once a thriving democracy, Venezuela is now an authoritarian state with one of the highest rates of poverty and emigration in the world. Many Venezuelans who fled to the United States now warn that they see the same signs of political and economic policies taking root in America.

The warnings from these countries are clear, socialist policies, even when implemented with promises of equality and fairness, lead to government overreach, economic collapse, and the loss of individual freedoms. America must heed these warnings and avoid the seductive but destructive path of socialism.

Another significant warning for America comes from Europe's decline into secularism. Many European nations were once bastions of christianity, sending missionaries across the globe and deeply embedding biblical values into their cultures and governments. Today however, Europe is overwhelmingly secular, with many churches standing empty, and christianity often regarded as irrelevant or outdated.

The secularization of Europe has had profound consequences. The rejection of christianity has led to a moral relativism where truth is subjective, and traditional values are seen as oppressive or outdated. This has resulted in societal fragmentation, rising crime, and a lack of shared values, which has weakened the social fabric.

America is following a similar trajectory. The rise of secularism in American culture, particularly among younger generations, is leading to a rejection of biblical values and a moral relativism that mirrors Europe. If America continues down this path, it will experience the same spiritual and societal decay that Europe is now grappling with. The church in America must take these warnings seriously and redouble its efforts to share the gospel, uphold biblical truth, and resist the encroachment of secularism.

The Warning from Israel: Turning from God Brings Judgment

The Bible provides perhaps the most compelling warning of all through the story of Israel. Time and again, Israel turned away from God, embracing idolatry and immorality, and as a result, they experienced God's judgment. The prophets of the Old Testament, such as Isaiah, Jeremiah, and Ezekiel, warned Israel that their rebellion against God would lead to destruction. And indeed, Israel was conquered by foreign powers, and the people were exiled from their land.

In many ways, America is walking the same path as ancient Israel. Despite its christian heritage, America has increasingly turned away from God, embracing secularism, immorality, and idolatry. The rejection of God's laws and principles has led to societal chaos, division, and moral confusion. If America continues to turn away from God, it should expect to face the same judgment that Israel experienced.

However, the story of Israel also offers hope. When the people repented and turned back to God, He showed mercy and restored them. America has the same opportunity for repentance and restoration if the church will rise up and lead the nation in returning to God.

The Warnings from the Rise of Totalitarianism

Another pressing warning comes from the rise of totalitarian regimes in the 20th century, particularly Nazi Germany and communist Russia. Both of these regimes rose to power through a combination of political manipulation, propaganda, and the suppression of dissenting voices. In both cases, the church remained largely silent or complicit as these regimes consolidated power, leading to the persecution of religious groups, the suppression of freedom, and the deaths of millions.

Today, many in America are sounding the alarm that the country is headed toward a similar authoritarianism. The increasing censorship of opposing viewpoints, the growing power of the state, and the suppression of religious freedoms are all signs that America is drifting toward totalitarianism. History has shown that when the church remains silent in the face of such threats, it only emboldens the forces of oppression.

These warnings from history and around the world are not meant to instill fear but to wake America up to the dangers it faces. There is still time to change course, but it will require action, particularly from the church. As America faces threats from within and without, the church must

Stand for Truth.The church must be a voice for truth in a culture that increasingly rejects absolute truth. This means boldly proclaiming biblical values, speaking out against injustice, and resisting the lies of secularism, socialism, and moral relativism.

Christians cannot afford to retreat from the political and cultural arenas. The church must be involved in shaping the laws and policies that govern society and advocating for the protection of religious freedom, life, and traditional values.

 Just as the prophets of old called Israel to repentance, the church must call America to turn back to God. This begins with prayer and revival within the church itself, followed by a bold and compassionate witness to the broader society.

The warnings from totalitarian regimes remind us that standing for truth may come with a cost. The church must be prepared for opposition and persecution, but it must remain steadfast in its mission to be a light in the darkness.

America stands at a critical juncture. The warnings from history, from other nations, and from Scripture are clear. If America continues down its current path, it will face the same fate as other nations that have fallen into tyranny, moral decay, and economic ruin. However, there is still time to change course. The church has a unique and powerful role to play in heeding these warnings, leading America back to God, and standing as a beacon of truth and righteousness in a darkening world.

The question is, Will the church rise to the occasion, or will it remain silent as the warnings go unheeded?

CHAPTER 15:

Give God A Reason

As America faces moral decline, political corruption, and cultural chaos, many christians hold fast to the belief that God will intervene. They pray for revival, hoping that God will save the nation from the consequences of its actions. However, throughout scripture, God's intervention is often preceded by a change in the hearts of His people. Before God acts, He often waits for a reason rooted in repentance, obedience, and a return to His ways.

This chapter challenges the church to "give God a reason" to act by taking responsibility for its spiritual condition and cultural influence. Rather than passively waiting for God to fix the nation, the church must rise up, repent of its complacency, and fulfill its role as salt and light in the world. The message is simple, God is ready to work, but He is calling His people to take the first step.

In Megan Basham's book Shepherds for Sale, she tells the story of a well known megachurch pastor whose journey from bold, biblical preaching to a more corporate driven, culturally relevant message highlights a significant issue plaguing modern evangelicalism. This pastor began his career with a clear vision, to preach the gospel without compromise and to take a firm stand on key moral issues facing society. Early in his ministry, he was known for addressing hot button topics such as the sanctity of life, the dangers of moral relativism, the importance of marriage, and the need for religious freedom in a secularizing world.

In the beginning, his sermons were unapologetically rooted in scripture. He boldly spoke out against abortion, warning his congregation that the culture of death taking hold in America was a direct affront to God's commandment to protect the innocent. He also delivered powerful messages on the importance of sexual purity, calling out the growing acceptance of same sex marriage and transgender ideology as clear departures from biblical teachings. His church, though not the largest at the time, had a reputation for standing firm on biblical truth, no matter the cost.

As the years passed, the pastor's church began to grow significantly. His sermons started gaining national attention, and his influence spread well beyond the walls of his congregation. He was invited to speak at conferences, featured on christian television, and even interviewed on mainstream media outlets. This newfound visibility, however, came with an increasing pressure to maintain the church's upward trajectory, both in attendance and financial success.

Basham describes how, as the church grew, so did the voices advising the pastor to be more strategic in his messaging. Public relations experts, media consultants, and even some key financial donors began suggesting that his strong stances on controversial issues might alienate potential churchgoers and draw unwanted criticism from the broader culture. Initially, the pastor resisted these suggestions, holding fast to the conviction that the church's role was to be a voice for truth in the world, regardless of how unpopular that truth might be.

However, as the church expanded and the budgets grew larger, the pastor found it harder to ignore the influence of these voices. Basham recounts how, slowly but surely, the pastor began to shift his focus. He stopped preaching as frequently on topics like abortion or biblical marriage. Instead, his sermons became more general, centered around self improvement, motivation, and how to live a happy and fulfilling life. Though these messages were still grounded in Scripture, they lacked the prophetic edge that had once defined his ministry.

The pastor's newfound caution wasn't limited to his sermons. He also began cultivating relationships with major corporations, many of which had openly embraced values that stood in direct opposition to christian teachings. These companies, however, were willing to sponsor church events, provide significant donations, and partner with the ministry for outreach programs. Basham explains how the pastor justified these partnerships as a way to reach more people for Christ, reasoning that if the church could gain a foothold in the culture, they could have a broader influence for good.

But this partnership came at a cost. When corporate sponsors or high profile donors objected to certain biblical teachings, particularly those that might be seen as offensive to secular audiences, the pastor's leadership team would often advise him to steer clear of those topics altogether. For example, during one particularly heated election cycle, the pastor was urged to avoid addressing the sanctity of life, despite the fact that abortion was one of the most hotly debated issues on the political stage. Basham describes how, to the dismay of many long time members, the pastor remained silent, opting instead for sermons on self care and emotional health.

Basham highlights how this shift created a growing sense of unease among the congregation. Members who had once been proud of their church's bold stance on moral issues now felt as though their spiritual leaders were more interested in keeping up appearances than standing for truth. Several members voiced their concerns, asking why the church was no longer addressing the cultural challenges that were affecting their daily lives, challenges like the growing hostility toward christian values in schools, media, and politics. These concerns, however, were met with carefully crafted responses from church leadership, who emphasized the importance of not alienating the broader community.

One of the most troubling developments, as Basham recounts, came when the church entered into a partnership with a major company that actively promoted ideologies contrary to christian teachings. This company had been at the forefront of championing LGBTQ rights and even contributed to pro abortion organizations. Despite this, the financial benefits and public relations boost from the partnership were deemed too valuable to pass up. Church members were told that by engaging with these corporations, they could "influence from within" and show the love of Christ to those who might otherwise never set foot in a church.

However, this engagement came at a price. The church was now firmly entrenched in a network of corporate interests, and the pastor became increasingly reluctant to speak out on moral issues that might jeopardize these relationships. Even when members of his own staff urged him to take a stand on critical issues, such as the government's encroachment on religious freedom, the pastor hesitated, citing the need to be "wise as serpents and gentle as doves." In reality, Basham argues, the church had become more concerned with maintaining its brand and its financial stability than with upholding biblical truth.

By the time the pastor realized the full extent of the compromises he had made, it was too late. His church, once a bastion of truth, had become little more than a corporate entity, focused more on growing its influence and protecting its financial interests than on shepherding the flock toward holiness. Basham paints a sobering picture of a church that has traded its prophetic voice for worldly success, and a pastor who, though well meaning, lost sight of the true mission of the church.

This story from Shepherds for Sale serves as a powerful illustration of the danger facing the modern church when it becomes too focused on financial and cultural success at the expense of biblical integrity. Basham's account demonstrates how easy it is for the church to become entangled in the world's systems and lose its distinctiveness as a voice for truth.

Throughout the Bible, God's mighty acts of deliverance, protection, and restoration often come after His people humble themselves, pray, and seek His face. One of the most well known passages, 2 Chronicles 7:14, captures this principle.

"If my people, who are called by my name, will humble themselves and pray and seek my face and turn from their wicked ways, then I will hear from heaven, and I will forgive their sin and will heal their land."

This passage makes it clear that God's intervention is conditional. It is not just the actions of a few that bring about change but the collective repentance and obedience of His people. God is willing to heal the land, but the church must give Him a reason to do so by turning back to Him in earnest prayer and repentance.

When Jonah preached to the city of Nineveh, the people responded with fasting, prayer, and repentance. As a result, God spared the city from the destruction He had planned, Jonah 3. The key here is that God was moved by the actions of the people, their humility, and their willingness to change.

Time and again, when Israel strayed from God's commands and faced judgment, God's mercy was extended only when the people repented. In the book of Judges, the cycle of disobedience, punishment, repentance, and deliverance is repeated over and over. God waited for His people to cry out before He acted.

Even in the New Testament, Jesus's ministry was marked by a call for repentance, Matthew 4:17. Before the Kingdom of God could break into the world through His ministry, there was a call for people to change their hearts and turn back to God.

The American church, in many ways, has become complacent. It has allowed itself to be seduced by comfort, convenience, and cultural relevance, often at the expense of biblical truth and obedience. While praying for revival is important, revival will not come without repentance. Too often, christians look at the problems in society, political corruption, immorality, and injustice, and ask God to fix it, without realizing that the real problem may lie within the church itself.

In many cases, the church has compromised with the world by adopting secular values, tolerating sin, and refusing to stand boldly for truth. This compromise weakens the church's influence and blurs the lines between what is holy and what is profane. If the church is to give God a reason to act, it must first cleanse itself of the compromise that has dulled its spiritual power.

The church is called to be a house of prayer, Isaiah 56:7, but too often, prayer has been neglected or relegated to a last resort. Without prayer, the church loses its connection to God's heart and His will. If the church is to give God a reason to heal the land, it must return to the basics of spiritual discipline, including prayer, fasting, and study of scripture.

Many christians have disengaged from the culture, either out of fear or a belief that the problems are too overwhelming. However, the church is called to be a transformative force in society, not a passive observer. If the church is to give God a reason to intervene in America's decline, it must be willing to re engage with culture, politics, and social issues in a way that reflects the love, truth, and justice of God.

God has given the church the responsibility of being His representative on earth, to reflect His character and principles in every sphere of life. This is not just a spiritual responsibility, but a moral and societal one. The church must recognize that its role is not just to worship within the walls of a building but to actively engage the world, pushing back darkness and injustice wherever they are found.

Jesus calls His followers to be the salt of the earth and the light of the world , Matthew 5:13-16. Salt preserves, and light illuminates. This means the church is called to preserve moral standards, protect life, and shine the light of Christ in dark places. When the church fails to be salt and light, decay and darkness follow. Giving God a reason means fulfilling this role with integrity and courage.

The prophets of the old testament consistently called out for justice in the land. Isaiah, Jeremiah, and Amos spoke against the oppression of the poor, the corruption of leaders, and the moral decay of the people. Today the church must once again be a voice for justice, speaking out against the evils of abortion, and human trafficking. God cares deeply about these issues, and the church must take a stand.

The church's mission is to make disciples of all nations, Matthew 28:19. Evangelism and discipleship are not optional, they are central to the church's calling. By spreading the gospel and making disciples, the church gives God a reason to bless its efforts and bring spiritual renewal to the nation.

While the church as a whole must repent and turn back to God, revival begins in the hearts of individuals. Each christian has a role to play in giving God a reason to act. This means taking personal responsibility for one's spiritual life, relationships, and actions.

Just as nations are judged by their collective sin, individuals are judged by their personal sin. Every christian must examine their own heart, confess their sins, and seek to live a life that honors God. This personal repentance is the first step in giving God a reason to move.

The family is the foundation of society, and strong christian families are essential to the health of the church. Raising children in the faith, strengthening marriages, and upholding biblical principles in the home are all ways that christians can give God a reason to bless the nation.

While personal repentance is important, collective action is also necessary. Christians must come together in prayer, service, and activism to address the moral and social issues facing the nation. This might mean organizing prayer rallies, volunteering at crisis pregnancy centers, or advocating for biblical values in the public square.

Throughout history, when God's people repented, sought His face, and acted according to His will, He responded with revival and renewal. From the great awakenings in America to the Welsh revival in the early 20th century, God has shown that He is eager to pour out His Spirit when His people are ready. The question is, Will the church in America give Him a reason to do so?

Revival will not come without repentance. Healing will not come without humility. Transformation will not come without obedience. The church must rise from its complacency, confess its sins, and return to its first love. Only then will God have a reason to heal the land, bring revival, and restore the nation.

The time for waiting is over. America is in desperate need of healing, but that healing will not come unless the church takes responsibility for its own spiritual condition. God is ready to act, but He is waiting for His people to give Him a reason. This chapter calls every christian, every church, and every believer to take up the mantle of responsibility and be the catalyst for the change they wish to see.

In this crucial moment in history, the church must not stand idly by. Now is the time to pray, to repent, to engage, and to give God a reason to pour out His mercy, grace, and healing power on a broken nation.

Conclusion

As we come to the end of this journey, the message of this book should be clear, silence is no longer an option. We are living in a time when the stakes couldn't be higher, and the cost of our passivity is becoming painfully evident. The church, once a moral compass and a powerful voice for truth and justice, has been reduced to a whisper in the face of mounting evil. But it doesn't have to stay that way.

We've walked through the history of America's founding, how biblical principles once guided this nation's course, and how that grounding gave rise to unprecedented freedom and prosperity. We've explored how the church, over time, has retreated from public discourse and allowed secular ideologies to take the wheel. From the legalization of abortion to the erosion of personal freedoms, from the rise of Marxism in our institutions to the dangerous lawlessness in our streets, the symptoms of a sick nation are all around us. And like in Nazi Germany, much of this has happened while the church remained silent.

The Bible tells us that faith without works is dead, and yet many in the church have settled for a passive faith, satisfied with piety over action. But there is no virtue in indifference. Prayer, though essential, cannot replace the need for bold, courageous steps in the public square. It's time to move beyond the walls of our churches, beyond the comfort of our pews, and re engage with the world around us. The Bible doesn't call us to retreat from the culture, but to transform it.

We cannot afford to stand idly by while our freedoms are stripped away, while innocent lives are lost, and while the moral fabric of our society unravels. Every moment of silence gives power to the very forces we should be resisting. History has shown us, time and time again, that when good people do nothing, evil prevails. And right now, we are watching evil take root in every corner of our society, unchecked by the voices that should be the loudest.

But this is not the end of the story. There is hope. Throughout this book, we have acknowledged the problems, but now it's time to embrace the solution. We are the solution. The church, if it finds its voice again, can be the force that turns this nation back toward righteousness. We can still reclaim the foundations that made this country great, but it requires action, bold uncompromising action.

We must engage in the political process, vote with our values, and hold our leaders accountable. We must take an active role in our communities, standing up for what is right even when it's unpopular. We must speak truth in love, knowing that our tone will never be accepted by those who prefer lies. The world will call us mean spirited, intolerant, even hateful, but it's time we cared more about God's judgment than the world's opinion.

The cost of silence has already been too high, but the cost of continuing to say nothing will be even greater. We cannot be the generation that watched America fall and did nothing. We must be the generation that took a stand, that spoke up when it mattered most, and that refused to let evil have the last word.

So, as you close this book, I ask you, what will you do next? Will you remain silent, or will you speak out? Will you retreat into comfort, or will you confront the culture with the truth of God's Word? The choice is yours, but I hope you choose courage. I hope you choose action. I hope you choose to break the silence. Because the future of this nation depends on it..

The End